Financing
the
Future

The Canadian Institute for Economic Policy has been established to engage in public discussion of fiscal, industrial and other related public policies designed to strengthen Canada in a rapidly changing international environment.

The Institute fulfills this mandate by sponsoring and undertaking studies pertaining to the economy of Canada and disseminating such studies. Its intention is to contribute in an innovative way to the development of public policy in Canada.

Canadian Institute for Economic Policy
Suite 409, 350 Sparks St., Ottawa K1R 7S8

Financing the Future

Canada's Capital Markets in the Eighties

Arthur W. Donner

Canadian Institute for Economic Policy

The opinions expressed in this study are those of the author alone and are not intended to represent those of any organization with which he may be associated.

ISBN 0-88862-568-5 cloth
ISBN 0-88862-567-7 paper

6 5 4 3 2 1   82 83 84 85 86 87

Canadian Cataloguing in Publication Data

Donner, Arthur W., 1937-
  Financing the future

1. Money market - Canada.   2. Capital - Canada.
3. Finance - Canada.   I. Canadian Institute for
Economic Policy.   II. Title.

HG655.D66 *1982*   332'.04152'0971   C82-094501-3

61,489

Additional copies of this book
may be purchased from:

James Lorimer & Company, Publishers
Egerton Ryerson Memorial Building
35 Britain Street
Toronto, Ontario M5A 1R7

Printed and bound in Canada

Contents

Tables

Foreword

The focus of this study is on the workings of capital markets in Canada in the 1980s, a decade of expected slow economic growth, high inflation and large current account deficits. The author, Arthur Donner, shows how energy, interest rates and inflation are at the core of capital market issues in Canada.

The institute is publishing this study to encourage public discussion of the issues related to the functioning of our financial institutions at a time of growing economic uncertainty. However, as with all our studies, the opinions expressed here are those of the author and do not necessarily reflect those of the institute.

Roger Voyer
Executive Director
Canadian Institute for Economic Policy

Preface

This study was prepared and essentially completed before the pervasive nature of the 1981-82 world oil glut and the international slump became clear. The oil glut and the serious international slump could possibly change the timing of some of the pressures identified in this study. For example, the heavy energy-oriented demands for project financing in Canada will clearly be delayed for some time, though the inventory of energy projects will be reactivated once real oil prices begin to rise again. Under the pressure of harsh economic policies in virtually all countries, inflation is moving down, though high real interest rates and unusually variable interest rates are expected to dominate the financial markets for some time to come. Canada's policy makers could very well alter the present tight economic measures and become more concerned about unemployment than inflation in 1983. A change in this direction could alter their policy stance vis-à-vis support of the Canadian dollar.

The author was fortunate to have the advice and critical comments of a number of friends and colleagues. Harry Baumann, Myron J. Gordon, Mel Kliman and Douglas D. Peters read drafts of the entire manuscript, and also offered valuable advice and criticisms during the course of its preparation. David Good and Wendy Carter also reviewed an early version of the study. The author was also fortunate to have had the opportunity of discussing many of the public policy dilemmas identified in the manuscript with Robert Rabinovitch. Abe Rotstein and the Honourable Walter Gordon not only inspired this second look at Canada's financial system, but also provided valuable insights into the public policy issues. Finally, Charles Casement was a patient and precise editor. Needless to say, while I am indebted to all of these people, they are in no way responsible for any errors or omissions found in the study.

While my children, Elizabeth and Simon, had little to do with the preparation of this manuscript, this study is dedicated to them with the hope that in some small way it might inspire at least one of them to consider the "dismal science" as a worthwhile career.

Introduction

The major concern of this study is the functioning of the Canadian capital markets in the turbulent 1980s. These markets encompass a series of financial institutions and interrelated financial markets through which funds are transferred from net savers to net spenders. It is through their important intermediary role that the capital markets are integrated into the organization of the entire economy, and thus they cannot be completely isolated from the analysis of such macroeconomic phenomena as economic growth, inflation and unemployment, and indeed from macroeconomic policies. The study's primary objective is to review a series of particular capital markets issues which will likely present significant challenges to economic policy makers in Canada in the 1980s.

Since there are so many different kinds of financial institutions and markets operating within the financial system, obviously this brief overview must be selective by focusing on challenges that relate most directly to public policy concerns. Seven capital markets issues have been selected which meet the twin criteria of having significant real economic impacts and, as well, involving public policy making. The topics discussed in this study by no means exhaust the total range of important capital market concerns for the 1980s. Inflation and energy concerns, and their impacts on the capital markets, are at the centre of the issues that are explored in the study.

Chapter 2 considers the theoretical and practical relationship between inflation and capital markets institutions. Most economists believe that inflation will continue to be an ongoing problem for the economies of the Western world in the 1980s and therefore that financial institutions will continue to respond to the effects of inflation. There are a wide number of institutional rigidities, customs and tax practices which make the impact of high inflation rather non-neutral on the economy, and this seems also to have been the case for the

Canadian capital markets. Aside from the question of the impact of inflation on interest rates, inflation probably also affects shifts of funds between financial institutions and markets and, of course, affects public policy decisions as well.

Chapter 3 considers the important changes central bank monetarism has imposed on the capital markets in Canada since 1975, with particular attention focused on the issues of high nominal and real interest rates, interest rate variability, exchange rate pressures and policy concerns. The question of whether or not Canadian interest rates can or should be decoupled from high and variable U.S. interest rates becomes central for Canadian policy makers.

Chapter 4 focuses on the special kinds of problems involved with the financing of large energy projects in an inflationary environment, where it is also difficult to raise long-term funds. Canadian governments and businesses have always been involved in the financing of megaprojects, but the expected wave of project financing in the 1980s is particularly heavy, and unusually centralized in Alberta and in the other western provinces. Financing for megaprojects will also be complicated because governments are involved in many different ways, and often there are overlapping domestic and international government jursidictions. More often than not, governments tend to delay the approval of projects, and in the process these delays increase the costs of the projects. Two other critical issues which are discussed in this chapter relate to whether or not the Canadian economy will generate a sufficient supply of domestic savings to finance these large projects, and, as well, whether the capital markets will be able to identify and coerce the appropriate supplies of risk capital for such projects.

Chapter 5 explores the ramifications of the Canadianization goal for the financial markets and indirectly for the economy. As discussed in this chapter, Canadianization involves the conversion of ownership or control of non-residential equity located within Canada. In order for the Canadianization program actually to be successful, it must involve some repatriation of capital abroad. But the balance of payments impact of an external repatriation of capital is usually immediately negative for the Canadian dollar, as witnessed by the heavy outflows of capital during the first six months of 1981. Indeed, the balance of payments impacts from such Canadianization transactions are identical to the effects that can occur through a shift of indigenous Canadian-controlled investment abroad. The crux of this is the fact that Canadianization and/or any other policy generating flights of capital out of Canada would depress the external value of the Canadian currency.

This chapter also considers the conditions under which a spontaneous Canadianization trend would emerge and also provides an estimate of how much further Canadianization would be required in order to achieve the National Energy Program's goal of 50 per cent Canadian ownership of the oil and gas industries. As long as the balance of payments position continues to be so fundamentally weak, and as long as Canada's inflation rate is in excess of that in the U.S., one should not expect too much ''spontaneous'' Canadianization to occur.

Substantial rises in the international price of crude oil in the 1970s spurred on a related shift in domestic terms of trade. This in turn resulted in a shift of economic and financial power to western Canada which is expected to continue on in the 1980s. Some of the financial ramifications of these economic shifts are explored in chapter 6.

Unfortunately, interregional financial flow data are very sketchy and are simply not very helpful for the purposes of analysing this question. But the financial ramifications of these economic shifts can be considered indirectly by focusing on regional trade changes which have occurred over the 1970s. The chapter also considers such questions as economic and financial power, and the fiscal and political effects generated within the country from such large pools of savings accruing to western governments. The Alberta government is clearly the beneficiary of some of these effects and it has set aside part of its resource-based revenue into the Alberta Heritage Trust and Savings Fund. The Saskatchewan government also has a Heritage Fund, which reached about $1 billion in 1981. Such funds, particularly the Alberta Heritage Fund, are growing very rapidly and potentially could be used as a means of attracting investment into the western provinces, though so far this has not been done.

Chapter 7 focuses on Canada's ailing housing industry, and highlights the adverse coming together of a series of external economic events (particularly high mortgage rates) with ill-conceived provincial and federal government policies (particularly rent controls). Once again the problems that emerged for Canada's housing industries in the 1970s seem likely to remain in place in the 1980s. The chapter also focuses on high real mortgage costs, the uneven incidence of monetary restraint across different cities in Canada, and the limited degree to which creative mortgages are the answer for this industry's problems.

A major revamping of the private and public pension fund system may be the outcome of a series of studies, commissions and federal-provincial bodies which reviewed this issue. The material in chapter 8 considers some of the major challenges which have surfaced with respect to shortcomings of the existing pension system. In one way or another, high inflation and high interest rates are at the centre of the policy dilemmas. The chapter reviews the funding of Canadian social security plans (particularly the Canada Pension Plan), the impact of social security savings on national savings, real rates of return to private pension plans, indexing concerns with respect to private pension benefits, and the mix of assets private pension plans may encounter in the 1980s.

Capital Markets and Financing Investment in the 1980s

1

Capital Market Institutions and Transactions

This chapter briefly describes Canada's capital market institutions and provides an example of their financial interdependence in 1969 and 1979 using financial flow-of-funds accounting statistics. This chapter also considers the broader question of how Canada will likely finance its future capital spending requirements and suggests shifts in various saving propensities and changes in the flow of funds which will be necessitated because of heavy private sector capital requirements in the 1980s.

Any institution or financial market that helps channel funds from savers to spenders is providing a financial intermediary service, and hence is part of the capital market. In Canada the financial intermediaries include deposit-gathering institutions, public financial institutions (including governments in their intermediary roles), the Bank of Canada, the private savings and investment funds, contractual savings institutions, and the social security system.

In practical terms, the funds transfer process necessitates the creation of legal documents which become the financial instruments and claims that are traded. The typical transaction involves the exchange of money — the key financial instrument — for other kinds of instruments, such as common stocks, preferred stocks, bonds, mortgages, debentures, short-term notes, and deposit certificates. The borrower must create one or more of these types of claims as a liability against itself and then sell it to some lender.

In fact, however, a direct exchange from the ultimate borrower to the ultimate lender occurs infrequently. Because of the complexity of the economic system, the net transfer of funds within the capital market from surplus to deficit units generally occurs circuitously. It is through this indirect process and through the matching up of the different term preferences of savers and borrowers that financial institutions carry out their important intermediary role. Savers (or the suppliers of funds) often prefer to purchase financial claims which are short-term, liquid and offer a low degree of risk. Borrowers, on the other hand, tend to prefer long-term debt, such as mortgages and bonds. The differences in the maturity term requirements of the borrowers and lenders are bridged by the financial intermediaries. The bulk of the liabilities of the intermediaries are short-term, such as deposits and term certificates at the banks and trust companies; whereas the largest proportion of the assets of these institutions are long-term, such as business loans, mortgages and bonds.

The data set out in Table 1-1 trace the movement of funds from the ultimate savers in our economy to the ultimate spending sectors, and succinctly highlight the intermediary roles of the various capital market bodies. The flow-of-funds statement is the financial counterpart of an economic input-output table which is used to analyse changes in real production relationships. Obviously, any serious disruption of the flows of funds either between Canada and the rest of the world, or within the various regions of Canada, or indeed even between major financial sectors, must have an impact on the real economy through the savings and investment decisions which ultimately affect production and employment. The capital markets issues examined in this study were chosen because of their important spillovers into the real economy. In particular, the real spillover effect can be seen most directly in the chapters dealing with public and private pension funds, the financing of energy megaprojects, the Canadianization of industry, the mortgage market, and changes in the regional flows of funds in recent years.

The flow of funds presented in Table 1-1 shows the aggregate flows of savings for each major sector of the economy, and the net flows of funds that move from one sector to another, during two calendar years, 1969 and 1979. The figures in the "lending or borrowing" columns illustrate whether a particular sector was a net lender or a net borrower within this financial system. The entries in this column add up to zero, since what one sector borrows, another sector must be lending. Funds are also transferred between units within a sector, but these should not show up in these statistics.

As these data illustrate, the major source of gross savings in Canada in 1979 were individuals and unincorporated businesses which generated 41 per cent of all savings, followed by non-financial corporations which provided 38 per cent of gross savings. In 1979 the federal government was a large dissaver and a large borrower,

TABLE 1-1

FINANCIAL FLOWS BY SECTOR, 1969 AND 1979

	1979			1969		
	Gross Savings		Net Lending (+)	Gross Savings		Net Lending (+)
Sector	$ m	% of Total	or Borrowing (−)	$ m	% of Total	or Borrowing (−)
Persons & unincorp. business	26,465	41.1	12,777	5,535	28.9	1,616
Non-fin. corps	24,176	37.6	−7,281	6,799	35.5	−2,189
Non-fin. govt enterprises	3,243	5.0	−6,197	807	4.2	−1,326
Monetary authority	5	0.0	−1	1	0.0	−2
Chartered banks	934	1.5	622	180	0.1	109
Near banks	141	0.2	−41	27	0.1	−3
Insurance cos & pension funds	68	0.1	−247	18	0.0	−64
Other private fin. insts	607	0.9	508	159	0.1	138
Public fin. insts	14	0.0	−466	4	0.0	−51
Federal govt	−8,084	−12.6	−9,170	1,570	7.9	1,019
Prov. & local govts & hospitals	8,609	13.4	2,038	2,356	12.3	−391
Social security funds	2,734	4.2	2,734	1,113	5.8	1,113
Rest of world	5,636	8.7	5,098	1,079	5.6	917
Residual error	−187	−0.3	−374	−443	−2.3	−886
Total	64,361			19,142		

Source: Statistics Canada, *Financial Flow Accounts* (Cat. No. 13-002) First Quarter, 1980, Table 1-4 and *Financial Flow Accounts*, vol. II (Cat. No. 13-563), Table 2-8.

although the opposite was the case a decade earlier. In 1979 net borrowings by the federal government accounted for about three-quarters of the total net loans offered by persons and unincorporated business. Non-financial corporations and non-financial government enterprises also were significant net borrowers in 1979.

These statistics illustrate that the financial intermediaries (chartered banks, near banks, insurance companies and pension funds) provide only a rather small amount of saving and net lending. While this is true, its meaning must be understood within the context of the statistical definitions used in flow-of-funds analysis. Gross savings are the funds generated by not spending one's income. Thus, the savings of the banks are comprised of capital consumption allowances and retained earnings which in aggregate amounted to $934 million in 1979. Chartered bank net lending ($622 million in 1979) is the amount left over after the acquisitions of real capital in the banking sector are subtracted from gross savings. This figure, in turn, is approximately equal to the difference between the accumulation of assets and the accumulation of liabilities by banks.

Of course, the gross financial flows of borrowing and lending that flow through the chartered banks and other financial intermediaries, to and from other sectors, are much greater than these figures suggest. As already noted, intermediaries borrow from one group and use the money to lend to another. In the course of doing that, assets and liabilities are created in amounts much larger than the net inter-sectoral flows suggest.

Finally, these capital market institutions are taking on an ever-growing role within the economy as direct purchasers of services and capital equipment, and also as direct employers. Indeed on an output or real production basis, the finance, insurance and real estate industries expanded by about 63 per cent between 1971 and 1980, far in excess of the expansion of all other industrial sectors in Canada. In comparison, output in the manufacturing industries expanded only 33 per cent, while production in the public and defence sectors, as well as the construction sector, each expanded only 31 per cent. In 1980 the same finance, insurance and real estate sector employed about 550,000 workers, which represented about 6 per cent of non-agricultural employment in Canada. In 1973 the percentage of non-agricultural employment centred in the financial services industries was only 5 per cent. The main point is that the financial services sector of the Canadian economy will likely continue to outperform the economy in general as a provider of real services in the 1980s.

4

Financing Canada's Investment Requirements in the 1980s

Will the savings and investment flows that will emerge in coming years be of sufficient magnitude to support Canada's future capital needs? Several medium-term projections of the Canadian economy are available which shed some light on Canada's future investment needs. But it is important to realize that the simple task of matching up gross savings with gross investment represents only part of the story. The matching problem is far more complicated in its microeconomic dimension, requiring information on term to maturity, risk preference of the lenders and other characteristics of large project financing.

But before these medium-term forecasts of investment flows are considered, two points deserve specific attention. One is fairly obvious, while the other is less so. First, the volume of Canadian savings and investment that will be required and/or generated is a function of both the macroeconomic performance of the Canadian economy as well as future policies concerning savings and investment. That is, the more rapidly the Canadian economy grows over the next decade, the greater the volume of savings and investments that will be generated. As well, since GNP growth also depends upon the average rate of increase in prices, a higher future inflation rate will result in a faster growth of GNP and, of course, a faster rate of increase in aggregate saving and investment.

In this regard, it is important to note that none of the studies or projections cited suggest that the Canadian economy will grow very rapidly in real terms. These projections, if realized, suggest troubles ahead for Canadian policy makers since the energy investment in these projections can be considered largely as autonomous expenditures. Therefore, the financial and real strains on the Canadian economy in the 1980s will increase because of the expected reduction in Canada's long-term real economic growth potential.

There is, of course, some controversy as to the true scale of future energy investment requirements. The financial press has been vocal about its concerns that the massive scale of the megaprojects alone would swamp the Canadian financial markets, and provide both a real and a financial crowding-out effect on other types of expenditures. Indeed, it is not often realized that the potential scale of energy investment in Canada relative to GNP is in fact greater than that of other OECD countries. This represents an important second dimension in any review of Canada's economic and financial prospects.

For example, Waverman and Donner[1] noted in 1981 that the energy share of total investment in the 1980s in Canada will not only be large but it will also likely exceed the proportions of any other OECD country. Their main conclusion was that the energy investment adjustment in Canada, assuming these demands can be treated as autonomous, will be much greater for Canada than for other Western countries. Table 1-2, taken from their study, highlights the disproportionate energy investment thrust in Canada relative to the other Western countries.[2]

The statistics set out in Table 1-3 cite a series of aggregate projections of Canada's investment requirements (or savings) relative to GNP for various time periods. These projections were made by the Economic Council of Canada, Darryl G. Waddingham of the Royal Bank, and Informetrica, the Ottawa consulting firm. They all point to a likely increase in the aggregate ratio of investment to GNP in the years ahead (to 25 per cent or so) and, as well, to the growing share of investment and GNP that will be allocated to energy developments.

A related issue concerns the prospective size of Canada's energy investment requirements in future years. Projections of the amount of funds that might be required have surfaced from many different organizations in the recent past. Four separate projections are provided in Table 1-4. It is difficult to compare these projections against each other because their time periods were not identical and the type of projects considered were not necessarily the same; nevertheless the sums of money involved in most cases seem very impressive. The Major Projects Task Force, for example, estimates that during the 1980s and 1990s Canada will have to raise about $431 billion to finance energy and non-energy megaprojects. Informetrica estimates the capital needs for 135 energy and non-energy projects at $120 billion, while the Royal Bank's study estimated that Canada would require about $500 billion at 1980 prices for investment over the last two decades of the century.

Future Sources of Gross Savings in Canada

What about the sectoral distribution of savings needed to finance these large-scale investments in the 1980s? In a strict identity sense, savings must equal investments in a closed economy, and the same definition holds for their respective ratios to GNP. But on a sector-by-sector basis, policy makers must be concerned about whether Canada will rely more heavily on foreign funds in the future than it has in the past, and whether a general increase in investment requirements can only be financed if new tax incentives are provided, and so on.

6

TABLE 1-2
INTERNATIONAL PROJECTIONS OF ENERGY INVESTMENTS, 1985, 1989

	Actual 1970		Actual 1979			Estimated 1985			Estimated 1989		
	%²	%³	$¹	%²	%³	$¹	%²	%³	$¹	%²	%³
US	1.9	13.5	81.0	3.4	20.9	117.1	4.4	24.3	127.2	4.4	25.1
Canada	3.4	15.3	11.8	5.2	23.3	20.4	7.8	31.5	22.5	7.9	31.4
Japan	1.8	5.1	20.0	2.0	5.8	57.4	4.4	14.4	72.7	4.5	14.7
EEC	1.5	6.9	42.2	1.8	8.9	44.5	1.6	7.3	48.5	1.6	7.2
Total			155.0	2.6	12.3	239.4	3.5	14.1	270.9	3.4	15.6

Notes: [1] Energy fixed capital formation, 1979 US $ billion.
[2] Energy supply investments/Gross national product (GNP).
[3] Energy supply investments/Gross fixed capital formation.

Source: Leonard Waverman and Arthur Donner, "Investments in Energy Supply Industries and the Economy of the OECD" (Paper prepared for the OECD/IEA, Toronto, May 1981), Table 15.

TABLE 1-3

PROJECTIONS OF INVESTMENT TO GNP RATIOS, CANADA—VARIOUS STUDIES

(%)

	1980	1985	1990	2000	1980 -85	1986 -90	1991 -95	1996- 2000	Cumu- lative 1979- 2000
1. Business investment as % of GNP									
(a) Budget with no alternative investment	15.9	18.2							
(b) Budget with alternative investment	15.5	18.2							
Gross investment as % of GNP									
(a) Budget with no alternative investment		23.9	25.5						
(b) Budget with alternative investment	23.6	25.6							
2. Gross investment (real terms) as % of GNP									
Base case: no large energy projects	22.6	24.8	25.4						
Energy investment as % of total investment	22.6	23.5	24.3						
Base case: no large energy projects	25.3	32.3	33.0						
Base case: no large energy projects	25.3	28.6	29.9						

	1980	1985	1990	2000	1980-85	1986-90	1991-95	1996-2000	Cumulative 1979-2000
3. Energy investment as % of GNP					5.9	7.3	8.4	9.4	
Energy investment as % of total investment					27.4	31.8	34.8	39.4	37.8
4. Gross investment as % of GNP	22.7	24.7	24.6	25.8					

Sources: 1. B.D. Eyford et al, "An Assessment of the Impact of the Federal Budget on the Canadian Economy," Economic Council of Canada Paper No. 185 (January 1981), pp. 85, 107, 115.
2. Economic Council of Canada, *A Climate of Uncertainty*, Seventeenth Annual Review, 1980, pp. 28, 47.
3. Darryl S. Waddingham, "The Canadian Balance of Payments to the Year 2000 with an Assessment of the Impact of the Polar Gas Pipeline Project" (November 1979).
4. Informetrica, "The Canadian Economy to 2000: Assumptions and Summary Post-Workshop 1980 Forecast" (June 12, 1980).

TABLE 1-4
VARIOUS ESTIMATES OF MEGAPROJECT EXPENDITURES IN THE 1980S AND 1990S
($ billions)

Source	Amount	Time Frame	Type of Investment	Regional Focus
1. Royal Bank—Polar Gas (1980)	$1,402 (current price), $500 (1980 prices)	1979-2000	Energy projects only	
2. Informetrica (1981)	$120 (current price)	1980s	135 energy and non-energy projects	Eastern Canada 30%; Western Canada, including Yukon/NWT 70%
3. Major Projects Task Force (1981)	$431 (current and constant prices)	1980s and 1990s	Energy and non-energy projects	Atlantic provinces 10.1%; PQ 17.2%; Ont 11.3%; Man 2.0%; Sask 2.5%; Alta 17.7%; BC 12.6%; Yukon/NWT 15.1%
4. Royal Trust Task Force (1981)	$98.7 in major projects, of which $57.4 will be financed externally—74% debt, 26% equity	1981-1986	Mainly energy projects	

Sources: 1. Darryl G. Waddingham, ''The Canadian Balance of Payments to the Year 2000 with an Assessment of the Impact of the Polar Gas Pipeline Project'' (1980), part IV.
2. Informetrica, ''Review of Current and Likely Major Investment Projects in Canada'' (April 1981).
3. Major Projects Task Force, draft of chapter 4 (1981).
4. Royal Trust, ''Through A Glass, Darkly: A Medium-Term Canadian Perspective 1981-1986'' (November 1981).

To some extent a review of how investment was actually financed in recent years points to some prospective changes for the 1980s. In 1980, the latest full year for which data are available, 22.9 per cent of Canada's GNP was saved. This is well below the projected 25 per cent savings to GNP ratios suggested in the studies which are summarized in Table 1-3. As well, there have been considerable changes in the behaviour of savers in recent years. Savings as a percentage of personal disposable income (the personal savings rate) has increased from the 5 to 6 per cent range in the early 1970s to the 11 to 12 per cent range in recent years; that is, the household propensity to save has doubled. The main offsetting factor in the aggregate savings ratio has been a decline in the percentage of GNP accounted for by personal income and an increase in the income tax rate (that is, the ratio of income taxes to personal income). Most of these trends are set out in Table 1-5.

Another indication that savings behaviour has changed recently can be seen in the sectoral distribution of savings presented in Table 1-6. To simplify the analysis, several savings sectors have been grouped together. The share of total gross savings generated by persons and unincorporated business has increased appreciably over the past two decades, from less than 30 per cent in the mid-1960s to 40 per cent in 1979. It is interesting to note as well that this increased share is due to increases in net savings; the capital consumption allowances in the personal sector have actually contracted as a proportion of total savings since the 1960s.

In the corporate sector, sharp fluctuations in savings relative to GNP are common, as profits vary significantly over the business cycle. But in recent years the corporate share of savings has been quite high. While it used to be typical for governments to be net suppliers of savings, their roles have changed since the mid-1970s, particularly because of the budgetary problems faced by the federal government and the governments of the eastern provinces. However, with the substantial shift of funds underway to western provincial governments, this trend may be altering. Social security funds, which include the Canada Pension Plan (CPP) and the Quebec Pension Plan (QPP), have been an important source of savings in the past, although their share of total savings also began to decline in the 1970s.

Finally, in the second half of the 1970s the flow of savings originating from the foreign sector has again become quite significant in Canada. Foreign savings are required to finance Canada's deficit on its current account. Since 1974, the Canadian current account deficit

TABLE 1-5
SAVINGS AND INCOME RATIOS IN CANADA, 1962-80
(%)

	1962	1965	1968	1971	1974	1976	1977	1978	1979	1980
Gross savings/GNP	22.5	25.7	22.7	21.5	25.8	23.8	23.4	23.2	24.6	22.9
Personal savings/Personal disposable income (PDI)	5.6	5.5	5.6	5.8	10.1	10.8	10.6	10.9	10.5	10.2
PDI/Personal income	89.5	88.3	84.1	80.9	80.9	80.9	80.9	81.6	81.8	81.5
Income taxes/Personal income	7.1	8.2	10.6	13.7	13.8	13.5	13.5	12.9	12.9	13.4

Source: Statistics Canada, *National Income and Expenditure Accounts*, various issues.

TABLE 1-6

PROPORTIONAL SHARES OF TOTAL GROSS SAVING BY MAJOR SECTOR, SELECTED YEARS, 1962-79

(%)

	1962	1965	1968	1971	1974	1976	1977	1978	1979
Persons & unincorporated business:									
Gross saving	34.3	28.8	30.4	32.8	38.5	42.8	44.5	45.7	40.0
CCA	(17.2)	(15.0)	(16.0)	(15.2)	(12.0)	(13.3)	(13.9)	(13.7)	(12.4)
Net saving	(17.1)	(13.8)	(14.4)	(17.6)	(26.5)	(29.5)	(30.5)	(32.0)	(27.6)
Financial & non-financial corporations:									
Gross saving	41.9	38.9	42.1	40.4	33.2	34.7	39.6	40.6	37.7
CCA	(27.4)	(23.3)	(25.1)	(26.6)	(21.4)	(22.2)	(23.9)	(23.8)	(20.7)
Net saving	(14.5)	(15.6)	(17.0)	(13.8)	(11.8)	(12.5)	(15.6)	(16.8)	(17.0)
Government:									
Gross saving	17.1	22.9	19.8	17.0	20.1	5.5	2.8	−1.4	4.1
CCA	(9.6)	(8.5)	(9.4)	(9.9)	(8.1)	(8.8)	(9.5)	(9.6)	(9.0)
Net saving	(7.6)	(14.4)	(10.4)	(7.1)	(12.0)	(−3.3)	(−6.7)	(−11.0)	(−4.9)
CPP/QPP:									
Gross & net saving	—	—	6.1	6.3	4.7	4.8	4.6	4.4	4.0
Non-residents:									
Gross & net saving	8.0	8.0	1.6	−0.9	5.4	10.4	9.4	10.6	8.5

Source: Statistics Canada, *National Income and Expenditure Accounts*, various issues.

was in excess of $4 billion in every year with the exception of 1980, when the deficit fell to $2 billion. In 1976 and 1978 the contribution of foreign savings to the total flow of savings in Canada exceeded 10 per cent.

Prospective Capital Market Pressures, 1981-86

An interesting medium-term review of the kind of saving shifts required to finance investments in Canada between 1981 and 1986 was set out in a task force report published by the Royal Trust Company.[3] The Royal Trust study concluded that the net financial positions of major sectors in the Canadian economy will have to change rather dramatically in order to accommodate heavy energy investments and weakening government demands for funds between 1981 and 1986. The specific capital market projections were consistent with the direction of financial flows set out in the other medium-term economic projections discussed earlier in this chapter.

Three separate tables relating to the financial forecast are presented here since they succinctly highlight the potential shifts in saving and investment patterns that will likely occur, and these data also hint at the problems usually associated with dramatic changes in the direction of saving and investment flows.

The figures presented in Table 1-7 are similar to the data commented upon earlier in Tables 1-1 and 1-6. The primary sources for saving or dissaving (a sector's net financial position) were projected for five important sectors of the economy: the federal government, all other levels of government (including the CPP and QPP), the personal sector, the business sector (which includes government enterprises), and the foreign sector.

The major conclusions stemming from these projections can be summarized as follows:

- The federal government is expected to remain a net borrower of funds between 1981 and 1986, but the government deficit is expected to shrink both absolutely and relative to the size of Canada's future GNP.
- Other levels of government, including the social security funds, are expected to remain in a surplus lending position over the first half of the 1980s, although there is a slight reduction in the surplus expressed in terms of a projected ratio of future GNP.
- The personal sector is expected to continue as a net lender of funds over the next half-decade. Indeed, net personal savings are expected to increase as a percentage of GNP to 4.6 per cent between 1982 and

14

NET FINANCIAL POSITION OF MAJOR SECTORS IN THE ECONOMY, 1972-80, WITH PROJECTIONS TO 1986

Year	Federal Govt		Prov. & Munic. Govs & CPP & QPP		Persons[1]		Businesses[2]		Non-Residents	
	$ m	% of GNP	$ m	% of GNP	$ m	% of GNP	$ m	% of GNP	$ m	% of GNP
1972	−566	−0.5	647	0.6	2,870	2.7	−3,949	−3.8	667	0.6
1973	387	0.3	865	0.7	3,737	3.0	−5,155	−4.2	242	0.2
1974	1,109	0.8	1,686	1.1	5,551	3.8	−9,636	−6.7	1,999	1.4
1975	−3,805	−2.3	−244	−0.1	8,052	4.9	−8,541	−5.2	5,252	3.2
1976	−3,391	−1.8	169	0.1	5,814	3.0	−7,545	−4.0	4,388	2.3
1977	−7,303	−3.5	2,298	1.1	7,110	3.4	−8,664	−4.1	4,756	2.3
1978	−10,654	−4.6	3,700	1.6	10,022	4.4	−9,061	−3.9	5,299	2.3
1979	−9,213	−3.5	4,562	1.7	11,608	4.4	−12,206	−4.7	5,438	2.1
1980	−10,697	−3.7	4,714	1.6	14,902	5.1	−12,985	−4.5	2,799	1.0
1981e	−8,000	−2.4	5,150	1.6	13,148	4.0	−22,998	−7.0	9,446	2.9
1982f	−9,400	−2.5	5,203	1.4	18,036	4.8	−25,229	−6.7	8,011	2.1
1983f	−8,620	−2.0	5,390	1.3	18,540	4.3	−26,986	−6.3	6,464	1.5
1984f	−7,430	−1.5	6,430	1.3	19,240	3.9	−30,488	−6.2	7,922	1.6
1985f	−5,580	−1.0	5,860	1.0	27,690	5.0	−38,414	−6.9	10,612	1.9
1986f	−3,140	−0.5	6,580	1.0	31,799	5.1	−34,533	−5.5	8,154	1.3
Average										
1972-76	−1,253	−0.9	615	0.4	5,223	3.6	−6,975	−4.8	2,510	1.7
1977-81	−9,173	−3.5	4,085	1.5	11,358	4.3	−13,183	−5.0	5,548	2.1
1982-86	−6,834	−1.4	5,893	1.2	23,067	4.6	−31,330	−6.3	8,233	1.7

e estimate.
f forecast.

Notes: [1] Includes non-incorporated business.
     [2] Includes government enterprises.

Source: Royal Trust, "Through A Glass, Darkly: A Medium-Term Canadian Perspective 1981-1986" (November 1981).

1986, which is a somewhat higher percentage than during the preceding four years.

- The business sector, which includes government enterprises, is expected to triple its net borrowing requirements between 1980 and 1986. Financing these huge business investment requirements will be the primary challenge for the capital markets in the 1980s. As is discussed below, the requisite supply of corporate funding will depend upon the combined government sector easing out of the borrowing markets as well as upon a reallocation of future funds from the housing industry towards the corporate sector.
- The inflow of foreign savings is expected to decline as a proportion of GNP in the 1980s. This conclusion is no doubt one of the more difficult to evaluate, for it is clear that in a heavy business investment environment any deficiency of domestic savings could be overcome by additional borrowing abroad.

It should also be stressed that the projections in the accompanying tables summarize only the projected net financial position of these sectors; a significantly larger flow of funds occurs within these sectors, but these flows are netted out in the final projections. Thus, while the personal sector is expected to continue as a net lending sector, with respect to mortgage finance that sector both contributes and uses funds. In total, though, the personal sector is expected to continue to extend loans in excess of its borrowings.

These projections suggest that the Canadian financial markets will be preoccupied with a different set of issues between 1981 and 1986 than they have been in the recent past. In recent years the Canadian capital markets have focused heavily on the financing of government debt. The government debt market will still remain a problem area in the sense that in an era of high real interest rates federal, provincial and government agency long-term bonds are not attractive for investment purposes. While the projections point to a slight rise in the size of the personal sector's surplus that will be available for lending, the largest sectoral shift of funds will occur as the total government sector withdraws as a large-scale borrower in the capital market and in the process provides room for private investment. That is, as government sector borrowing shrinks relative to past ratios of GNP, this scaling-back permits the financing of larger-scale investment projects. If the shrinking of the government deficits proves too optimistic, then other borrowing sectors will likely find their investment programs more difficult to achieve.

The projections of strong business demand for funds set out in Table 1-8 is consistent with the megaproject theme which has been stressed in the present study. The Royal Trust report assumed that a total of $98.7 billion of energy-oriented project spending would occur between 1981 and 1986, and that $57.4 billion would have to be raised through external financing in the form of either new stock issues or new bonds.

It is also assumed that these major sectors will supply funds in 1986 in relatively the same way as occurred in 1980. As these data indicate, the net lending sectors dispose of their surplus funds by issuing consumer credit and extending loans, and through the purchase of financial assets such as treasury bills, short-term paper, mortgages, government and corporate bonds, and common stock. Based on this supply-of-funds framework, the potential supply of funds available for mortgage finance over the six years ending 1986, $152.7 billion, appears more than adequate in view of the likelihood of the continued weakness of housing demand.

But it is by no means clear that private business investment will be easily funded in coming years, since this requires financial institutions to shift their investment portfolios away from government and mortgage debt towards business investment. As noted earlier, there is sizeable room for such a major shift of funds, but dramatic changes such as these do not occur easily, especially if interest rates remain high in real terms.

Potential capital market strains are illustrated in the projections set out in Table 1-9. The business sector would require about $165 billion of equity to be financed between 1980 and 1986, and a substantial share of these funds (77 per cent) would normally be financed by the personal sector.

The Royal Trust report concluded that, based on traditional allocations of surplus savings, there exists the possibility of an excess supply of funds being available for government finance. That is, based on past trends, the capital marketplace would be willing to purchase about $22.6 billion of treasury bills, $62.2 billion of federal government bonds, $55.3 billion of provincial government bonds, and $14 billion of municipal bonds between 1981 and 1986.

But government deficits are expected to shrink, and therefore this excess supply of funds to governments will have to shift elsewhere. The non-financial corporations are projected to require about $252 billion of new financing between 1980 and 1986, while financial institutions have to raise about $60 billion in order to increase their equity positions in line with the future growth of their assets. Without

17

TABLE 1-8
PROJECTED ACQUISITION OF LOANS AND SECURITIES, 1980-86
($ millions)

	Consumer Credit	Loans	Treasury Bills	Short Paper	Mortgages	Federal Bonds	Prov. Bonds	Munic. Bonds	Corp. Bonds	Stocks
Bank of Canada	—	3	5,569	—	—	10,818	—	—	—	—
Chartered banks	34,922	107,356	8,883	169	22,501	2,959	577	181	4,581	8,905
Near banks	9,430	2,836	701	2,417	65,183	2,404	2,127	1,191	2,820	2,751
Life cos & pension funds	2,179	254	511	3,937	27,103	9,510	18,378	2,994	16,164	14,811
Other priv. fin. insts	5,122	19,470	1,412	3,720	6,560	3,334	2,151	804	2,744	5,015
Public fin. insts	—	9,432	167	499	13,632	673	5,900	448	1,079	1,003
Non-residents	—	6,367	1,035	2,868	1,234	5,550	19,920	2,124	12,650	5,306
Personal sector	472	—	4,343	2,073	16,529	26,957	6,220	6,275	3,028	127,602
Total	52,125	145,718	22,621	15,683	152,742	62,205	55,273	14,017	43,066	165,393

Source: Royal Trust, "Through A Glass, Darkly: A Medium-Term Canadian Perspective 1981-1986" (November 1981).

TABLE 1-9
PROJECTED DEMAND FOR AND SUPPLY OF FUNDS, 1980-86
($ millions)

Sector	Demand[1]	Supply[2]		Excess Supply (+) / Excess Demand (−)
Federal government	−42,170	T-bills	22,621	+42,656
		Bonds	62,205	
		Total	84,826	
Prov. & munic. govts	−34,615	Prov. bonds[3]	55,273	
		Munic. bonds	14,017	

Sector	Demand[1]	Supply[2]		Excess Supply (+) Excess Demand (−)
Business sector:				
Non-financial corps:				
To finance capital investment & inventories	−179,648	Stocks	(50,000)[6]	
To finance working capital	−71,859	Corp. bonds	165,393	
	−251,507	Loans[4]	43,066	
			75,000	
		Short paper[5]	3,000	
			286,459	
Financial institutions:				
Debt capital	−14,368			
Share capital	−45,574			
	−59,942			
Total business	−311,449		(171,066)[6]	(−140,383)[6]
			286,459	−24,990

Notes:
[1] Estimates for government and non-financial corporations from Table 1-7. Estimates for financial institutions based on assumption of 14 per cent p.a. growth in capital base, slightly faster than projected growth in total assets.
[2] Estimates based on data in the Royal Trust study.
[3] Excludes bonds purchased by public financial institutions.
[4] Of total loans, about half go to non-financial corporations.
[5] Of total short paper issued, about 20 per cent is by non-financial corporations.
[6] The figures in brackets are probably more realistic as they are based on some suggested concerns raised in the text of the Royal Trust report. That is, most of the $166 billion could be dissipated in payment for existing equity at higher prices, hence only about $50 billion might be available for new equity financing from the business sector.

Source: Royal Trust, "Through A Glass, Darkly: A Medium-Term Canadian Perspective 1981-1986" (November 1981).

the requisite redirection of savings, the potential supply of funds to the business sector could fall short of forecasted demands.

Assuming past trends, between 1981 and 1986 the identified lending sectors would be willing to allocate about $165 billion to common stocks, purchase $43 billion in bonds, and extend about $75 billion in loans. Based on these rough projections, the business sector would experience a shortfall of about $25 billion, which could be made up by shifting funds out of the government securities market. However, the Royal Trust report warns that the shortfall for the business sector could be more significant than the figure of $25 billion implies.

If, between 1981 and 1986, there is a substantial increase in equity prices, this could mean that much of the new funds flowing into common stock investments would be dissipated on existing rather than new equities. It might be more reasonable to assume that possibly at most $50 billion will be available for new equity investment over the six years ending 1986. If that is the case, there could be an "apparent" greater shortfall of funds for non-financial corporations. The projections in brackets in Table 1-9 suggest that the shortfall could amount to as much as $140 billion, a figure that does not seem quite as manageable as the original $25 billion.

However, these projections might understate the total sector shift of funds in another way. The Royal Trust study assumed a total expenditure on investment projects of about $98.7 billion between 1980 and 1986, of which $57.4 billion would be financed externally. This investment total could turn out to be on the low side. The Major Projects Task Force, for example, estimated an investment potential of $430 billion for the 1980s and 1990s. If the $430 billion figure is distributed equally over time, it works out to about $129 billion between 1980 and 1986, of which $74.9 billion would have to be raised externally.

In a sense all of this discussion is hypothetical since the capital markets will clear away any major surpluses of deficits so that institutional financing will flow in the required direction. The projections in Table 1-9 are simply used to illustrate, based on Canadian investment preferences prior to 1980, that there could be a surplus of funds available to government and an important shortfall of funds for private investment.

Conclusion

In summary, the projections cited in this chapter indicate that the successful financing of future large-scale business investment will require a substantial decline in total government borrowing in order to permit a diversion of funds from government bonds to corporate stocks and bonds, and some diversion of funds away from mortgage finance into business investment. The foreign sector will also have to make an important investment shift, from essentially purchasing provincial government debt towards the purchase of Canadian corporate bonds and common stocks. This latter shift may prove difficult — one simply cannot assume that non-resident investors will comfortably add bonds to their portfolios as long as the memories and problems associated with high "real" interest rates and Canada's high inflation rate continue. Canadian investors would normally have purchased as much as $153 billion worth of mortgages between 1980 and 1986, but Canada's housing industry will likely not expand very swiftly over this period; thus it may very well be that this type of redirection of foreign finance will also be important in the 1980s.

But aside from the fact that the capital markets will generate a clearing function, there are the following challenges which are subsumed in these aggregate projections:

- Although the personal sector will remain a net lending sector, individuals have accumulated in some cases large-scale debts based on increasing nominal values of their fixed assets, particularly houses. This game may essentially be over, and under a generally sluggish real growth medium-term economic outlook, a shift in the relative inflation rate between houses and other items in the consumer price index implies greater personal financing problems in the years ahead.

- High interest rates and a poor economic outlook have also forced non-financial corporations to increase their debt obligations relative to their equity base. There is much greater financial risk to industrial corporations and small businesses because of their highly-levered financial status. This additional risk is already recognized in the widening borrowing differential between government bonds and corporate bonds which has opened up since 1980.

- Although the Canadian chartered banks provide only an intermediary function, their financial health has become important with respect to the smooth growth of the capital market. Indeed, as pointed out in chapter 2, the banks' share of total business has probably increased as inflation has dried up the corporate bond market. But the chartered banks have recently experienced declines in their own capital-to-asset ratios. Unless these ratios increase in coming years, this may prove a constraint on the growth of their total assets and their total loans.

21

Inflation and its Impact on the Canadian Capital Markets   2

Inflation, Interest Rates and Various Spreads

Behind the concrete variables that determine the demand for and supply of financial assets, which in turn affect the health of the financial markets and the economy in general, is the ever-present influence of inflation and inflationary expectations. Classical economic theory has postulated a fairly direct and proportionate relationship between increases in the rate of inflation and increases in interest rates. But in fact the mechanism is thought to operate through changes in the public's expectations concerning inflation. While there is still considerable debate over how individuals formulate their inflationary expectations, it seems fairly clear that the prevailing rate of inflation has a significant impact on the expected rate of future inflation and consequently on interest rates in general.

Let us consider the following example. Suppose a lender is willing to make available loanable funds at a 3 per cent *real* interest rate. That is, he would accept $3 on every $100 lent out as adequate compensation if prices were expected to remain constant — he is interested in the real purchasing power of the interest. If, however, he expects a 7 per cent inflation rate to prevail over the next year, he will demand a *nominal* rate of interest of approximately 10 per cent. For every $100 loaned, he can now apply $7 back to the nominal value of his original asset to restore its real purchasing power. The remaining $3 is left over as a net return. By the same token, it is reasonable to assume that a borrower holds the same 7 per cent inflation rate expectation. Consequently the borrower would expect his income or his business revenue to grow by the same 7 per cent inflation rate, so that he can pay a 10 per cent nominal rate if it was worth a 3 per cent real rate to have the loan. This kind of thinking is a key part of the explanation for high interest rates in Canada in recent years.

In a broad sense this proportionate relationship between interest rates and inflationary expectations tends to be realized in the marketplace. But the relationship is neither as proportional nor as smooth as one would expect. There are long periods of time when high inflation rates tend to be undervalued in the capital markets and there are periods of time when they seem to be overvalued.

The incentives provided to the economy when real interest rates are normally positive in, say, the 2 to 3 per cent range, or alternatively sharply positive in the 3 per cent or greater range, or even zero or negative, vary quite substantially. This principle can be illustrated using the inflation and interest rate data set out in Table 2-1. The important calculation in this regard is the simple subtraction of the prevailing inflation rate from the existing nominal rate of return on the financial instrument. During the early 1970s, the real returns to mortgages, for example, were positive — in the 4 to 5 per cent range — and trust companies earned a comfortable spread in terms of their cost of money (the five-year guaranteed investment certificate [GIC] rate) and their return, using the conventional mortgage rate.

Inflation stepped up sharply in Canada between 1973 and 1975, to a peak rate of increase of 12 per cent during the fourth quarter of 1974, and mortgage rates shot up as well, but barely exceeding the inflation rate in 1974 and 1975. Thus during these three years, even without considering after-tax rates of return, the real mortgage rate fell, punishing lenders and providing a bonus to house purchasers. As inflation in Canada eased in 1976, fairly positive real rates of return were earned in the mortgage investment field, though once again sharp variations were to come in future years. It must be stressed that the returns to investing in mortgages are calculated as if only new investments are undertaken in every particular year. In fact, with the rise in mortgage rates generally, the market value of an existing mortgage instrument fell quite sharply.

Another factor affecting the availability of mortgage finance in any period is the willingness of traditional mortgage lending institutions to make these funds available. In essence, mortgage lending institutions are always considering their margin spread between the cost of raising funds and the returns from their mortgage investments. A rough approximation of this margin spread can also be seen in Table 2-1 as the simple difference between the five-year conventional mortgage rate and the five-year GIC rate. Since 1971 that spread ranged from a low of 116 basis points in the third quarter of 1973 to a peak of 530 basis points during the fourth quarter of 1981. But five-year mortgages were basically unavailable after 1980. Mortgages for three years or less were

TABLE 2-1
INFLATION, INTEREST RATE DIFFERENTIALS AND THE TERM STRUCTURE, 1971-81
(%)

Year & Quarter	Annual Rate of CPI Inflation	Chartered Bank Rates			Trust Co. Rates			GIC Non-Chequable Bank Rate Differential	Av. of 10 Industrials Less the Prime Rate Differential	Canadian Prime Less the US Prime Rate Differential	Long-Term Govt (10 yrs +) Less Short-Term Govt (3 mo.) Differential
		Bank Prime Lending Rate	Non-Chequable Savings Rate	Differential	Conventional Mortgage Rate	5-Year GIC Rate	Differential				
	(1)	(2)	(3)	(4)=(2)-(3)	(5)	(6)	(7)=(5)-(6)	(8)	(9)	(10)	(11)
1971 1	1.7	7.0	5.0	2.0	9.72	7.85	1.87	2.85	1.30	1.25	2.79
2	2.2	6.5	4.5	2.0	9.25	7.53	1.72	3.03	1.97	1.0	4.35
3	3.2	6.5	4.5	2.0	9.53	8.0	1.53	3.50	1.91	0.5	3.36
4	4.2	6.0	4.0	2.0	9.26	7.6	1.66	3.60	2.14	0.5	3.32
1972 1	4.8	6.0	4.0	2.0	8.93	7.05	1.88	3.05	2.21	1.25	3.45
2	4.3	6.0	4.0	2.0	9.16	7.62	1.54	3.62	2.3	1.0	3.61
3	4.8	6.0	4.0	2.0	9.41	7.95	1.46	3.95	2.39	0.5	3.94
4	5.2	6.0	4.0	2.0	9.3	7.75	1.55	3.75	2.25	0.25	3.40
1973 1	5.9	6.0	4.0	2.0	9.02	7.54	1.48	3.54	2.2	-0.25	3.22
2	7.3	7.0	4.5	2.5	9.3	7.87	1.43	3.37	1.4	-0.25	2.54
3	8.2	8.25	6.25	2.0	9.91	8.75	1.16	3.50	0.46	-1.5	1.64
4	9.0	9.0	6.75	2.25	10.02	8.67	1.35	1.92	-0.29	-0.75	1.21
1974 1	9.7	9.5	7.25	2.25	10.01	8.61	1.40	1.36	-0.52	0.75	1.67
2	10.7	11.0	8.75	2.25	11.26	9.66	1.60	0.91	-0.88	-0.5	0.28
3	11.0	11.5	9.25	2.25	11.85	10.31	1.54	1.06	-0.48	-0.5	0.73
4	12.0	11.0	9.25	1.75	12.0	10.36	1.64	1.11	-0.66	0.5	1.38

Year & Quarter	Annual Rate of CPI Inflation (1)	Chartered Bank Rates — Bank Prime Lending Rate (2)	Chartered Bank Rates — Non-Chequable Savings Rate (3)	Differential (4)=(2)-(3)	Trust Co. Rates — Conventional Mortgage Rate (5)	Trust Co. Rates — 5-Year GIC Rate (6)	Differential (7)=(5)-(6)	GIC Non-Chequable Bank Rate Differential (8)	Av. of 10 Industrials Less the Prime Rate Differential (9)	Canadian Prime Less the US Prime Rate Differential (10)	Long-Term Govt (10 yrs +) Less Govt (3 mo.) Short-Term Differential (11)
1975 1	11.7	9.5	7.25	2.25	10.95	8.78	2.17	1.53	0.49	1.0	1.91
2	10.5	9.0	6.5	2.5	10.99	9.22	1.77	2.72	1.62	1.75	1.84
3	10.9	9.0	6.5	2.5	11.52	9.8	1.72	3.30	1.94	1.25	1.52
4	10.1	9.75	7.25	2.5	11.97	10.13	1.84	2.88	1.4	2.25	1.06
1976 1	9.2	9.75	7.25	2.50	11.80	10.00	1.80	2.75	0.94	3.00	0.48
2	8.5	10.25	8.00	2.25	11.99	10.30	1.69	2.30	0.32	3.25	0.38
3	6.5	10.25	8.00	2.25	11.83	10.24	1.59	2.24	0.17	3.25	0.11
4	5.9	9.75	8.00	1.75	11.56	9.94	1.62	1.94	0.29	3.25	0.23
1977 1	6.8	8.75	6.25	2.50	10.25	8.78	1.47	2.53	0.08	2.50	0.97
2	7.6	8.75	6.25	2.50	10.38	9.05	1.33	2.80	-0.04	2.25	1.72
3	8.4	8.25	5.75	2.50	10.33	9.00	1.33	3.25	0.37	1.25	1.43
4	9.1	8.25	5.75	2.50	10.34	8.99	1.35	3.24	0.44	0.50	1.48
1978 1	8.8	8.25	5.75	2.50	10.31	8.85	1.46	3.10	1.69	0.25	1.85
2	8.9	9.25	6.75	2.50	10.43	9.29	1.14	2.54	0.70	0.75	1.03
3	9.3	9.75	7.25	2.50	10.31	9.00	1.31	2.25	0.14	0.75	1.36
4	8.7	11.50	9.00	2.50	11.26	10.00	1.26	1.00	-1.25	0.0	-0.82
1979 1	9.1	12.00	9.50	2.50	11.26	9.99	1.27	0.49	-1.48	0.25	-0.83
2	9.3	12.00	9.50	2.50	11.06	9.80	1.26	0.30	-1.71	0.25	-1.16
3	8.7	12.50	10.00	2.50	11.80	10.36	1.44	0.36	-1.65	0.25	-0.13
4	9.6	15.00	12.25	2.75	14.46	11.81	2.65	-0.44	-3.28	-0.50	-2.68

TABLE 2-1 continued

Year & Quarter	Annual Rate of CPI Inflation	Chartered Bank Rates			Trust Co. Rates			GIC Non-Chequable Bank Rate Differential	Av. of 10 Industrials Less the Prime Rate Differential	Canadian Prime Less the US Prime Rate Differential	Long-Term Govt (10 yrs +) Less Short-Term Govt (3 mo.) Differential
		Bank Prime Lending Rate	Non-Chequable Savings Rate	Differ-ential	Conven-tional Mortgage Rate	5-Year GIC Rate	Differ-ential				
	(1)	(2)	(3)	(4)=(2)−(3)	(5)	(6)	(7)=(5)−(6)	(8)	(9)	(10)	(11)
1980 1	9.4	15.00	12.00	3.00	13.50	11.57	1.93	−0.43	−1.65	−1.50	−0.64
2	9.6	13.75	12.50	1.25	13.99	11.96	2.03	−0.54	−1.46	−0.75	−0.16
3	10.5	12.25	9.25	3.00	13.44	12.06	1.38	2.81	−1.10	0.75	2.20
4	11.1	13.75	10.50	3.25	15.00	12.00	3.00	1.50	0.04	−4.00	1.10
1981 1	12.2	18.25	13.50	4.75	15.27	13.00	2.27	−0.50	−3.84	−0.25	−3.45
2	12.6	19.50	15.75	3.75	17.82	15.50	2.32	−0.25	−3.56	2.00	−3.47
3	12.7	22.75	19.00	3.75	21.30	17.50	3.80	−1.50	−4.81	2.25	−4.05
4	12.5	17.25	13.50	3.75	18.80	13.50	5.30	0.0	−7.20	1.50	−0.75

Note: The consumer inflation rates were calculated by averaging all of the quarterly index values, and then expressing the change relative to the same quarter one year earlier. Only the mid-quarter values of the various interest rates are reported.

Source: *Bank of Canada Review*, various issues.

The rates set out under columns 2, 3 and 4 represent a rough proxy of chartered banking profit spreads. Columns 5, 6 and 7 roughly represent the trust company incentive to invest in mortgages. Column 8 figures reflect trust company abilities to attract term deposits compared with the banks. Column 9 data reflect the corporate incentive to borrow in the long-term bond market compared with borrowings at the banks. Column 10 data are a measure of interest rate differentials between Canada and the U.S., while the statistics in column 11 are one measure of the term structure of interest rates for the federal government.

more prominent, and the interest rate spreads were about the same as the noted five-year spreads. In 1981 and 1982 most mortgages were renewed with terms of one year or less.

For much of the 1970s in North America the prevailing rate of inflation seemed to be in excess of the nominal yields earned on long-term bonds. Statistics not presented here plus data shown in Table 2-1 illustrate that real long-term yields (defined here as the difference between the yield on long-term bonds less the annual rate of increase in the consumer price index) were strongly positive in parts of the 1950s and 1960s and for a time were negative or practically zero in the 1970s.

A period of variable and high inflation seems to affect not only interest rates but also the institutions that gather deposits. For example, we tend to observe most interest rates rising with increases in inflation, though for various periods in the second half of the 1970s the trust companies, in particular, had their profit margins squeezed because of their inability to increase mortgage rates as quickly as their five-year GIC rate increases.

As well, the data in Table 2-1 illustrate some uneven effects on other short-term and long-term interest rates. The differential between long-term industrial bonds and the prime lending rate (column 9) narrowed and then became negative as inflation mounted through this period. The competition for funds, as represented by the trust company/chartered bank deposit rate differential (column 8), also narrowed from 360 basis points in 1971 to a negative in early 1980 and 1981.

If higher inflation rates had resulted in perfectly proportionate changes in the term structure, one would have expected the marginal effects of inflation to be approximately neutral across these financial institutions. Despite the fact that for both the banks and the trust companies the important cost of funds versus employment of funds interest differentials remained somewhat stable (see columns 4 and 7), the fact that the trust companies tend to tie their GIC rates to the conventional mortgage rate — an asset yield that adjusts somewhat unevenly — resulted in their becoming less competitive with the banks as the inflation rate rose.

Rising rates of inflation since the late 1960s, with recent Canadian peaks in 1975 and 1981, resulted in a general shortening of the term structure of all debt. The shortening of debt, of course, was related to lender uncertainty and the unwillingness of borrowers to commit themselves to long-term contracts at what were considered high rates. When capital markets respond imperfectly to current rates of inflation (this still may be rational, since markets react presumably not to current but to expected future inflation rates), there is greater lender uncertainty. This results in a greater emphasis on safety rather than on rewards associated with higher rates of return. Obviously those institutions that were able to match up their liability and asset maturities were least exposed to such risks. Since 1967, the chartered banks had the greatest matching flexibility of any of the financial institutions.

It is sometimes worthwhile to consider the extraordinary capital losses that rising interest rates impose on the market value of fixed-income securities, such as government or corporate bonds. For example, on June 15, 1974 the Government of Canada tapped the long-term bond market for $150 million with a bond which carried a coupon rate of 9.5 per cent and with a term to maturity of 20 years. During its first month of trading that particular issue had a market value of about $96.56 even though its original face value was $100.00. Indeed, during the first month of issue that security yielded 9.9 per cent to the investor or purchaser. Long-term government yields were fairly stable between 1974 and mid-1977, but following that period, long-term interest rates first rose about 120 basis points between the summer of 1977 and the summer of 1979, and then rose particularly sharply to a new and much higher peak level in 1981 at about 17 per cent. Since the market value of bonds moves inversely with interest rate movements, by May 1981 this particular bond was yielding 16.9 per cent to new purchasers and its existing market value had declined to $65.12. Thus between 1974 and 1981, holders of government bonds — private lenders, financial institutions, private pension plans, etc. — suffered about a 35 per cent loss in the market value of their capital. Indeed, the same situation holds in the case of any fixed rate of interest financial instrument, including mortgage interest rates. That is, over this period of rapidly rising long-term interest rates there was a substantial transfer of funds from lenders to borrowers, making lenders all the more ''gun-shy'' in an inflationary and high interest rate period. Mortgage lending institutions, such as trust companies, became much more aware of mismatches in the terms of their assets and liabilities.

By 1981 investor sentiment with respect to fixed-term bond instruments had soured quite noticeably; indeed, the financial press in Canada was continuously spreading doom and gloom reports concerning the demise of the long-term bond market. As long as interest rates, and inflation, remain at as high a level as they have attained in recent years there is no doubt that these prognostications could come true. But when, and if, the general rate of inflation in Canada decelerates, one should expect — possibly with a long delay — a return to much more open market financing by corporations and a general lengthening of the term of fixed income securities once again.

While it is impossible to isolate precisely the impact of the inflation process on the competition for funds, the following developments appeared to be associated with an almost quadrupling of inflation rates between 1971 and 1981.

It was in the post-1971 period when inflation accelerated that five-year conventional mortgages became commonplace. This was, of course, a rational response by lenders as they witnessed their capital assets shrink in value because of higher inflation. Indeed, on several occasions during 1980 and 1981 when short-term interest rates in Canada approached or surpassed 20 per cent, even three-year term mortgages became non-existent. Over the last several years, in particular, new house purchasers and those Canadians who have been rolling over their mortgages as they came due have been forced to accept very short-term mortgages of one to three years maturity, with very high interest rates. Indeed, many Canadians in recent years have been forced to make costly financial mortgage decisions vis-à-vis terms and interest rates, with little assurance one way or the other that their guesses would be accurate. These borrowers have, in fact, been forced by circumstances and very high interest rates to become financial speculators.

The Canadian government term structure of debt had shortened rather dramatically in the late 1970s. Up until the massive $12 billion financing of Canada Savings Bonds (CSBs) in November 1981 (at a record 19.5 per cent rate), the shortening took the form of a lesser reliance on CSBs and longer-term fixed interest bonds, with a greater reliance on shorter-term treasury bill and bond financing. With a shorter-term debt structure, the Canadian government was forced to come to the open market more frequently, and because of the additional burden of very high deficit levels in 1980 and 1981, this not only caused financial embarrassment for the government but was also a source of deterrence to the investment community. The huge 1981 CSB issue removed some of the government's bond market pressures in 1982.

The drying up of corporate borrowing via the open market, and the apparently greater reliance on the chartered banks, appeared to be associated with the higher inflation rates. Factors that tended to mitigate the corporate borrowing via the banks were a reliance on preferred stocks due to a favourable tax treatment of dividends, the sharper increase in bank prime lending rates vis-à-vis bond rates during parts of the past decade, and the widening interest rate differentials between Canada and the U.S., which at times (1975, 1977 and 1981) favoured borrowing in the U.S. marketplace.

Valuation and Tax Rate Implications of Inflation

As price inflation heats up, corporate balance sheet inventories increase rapidly in value. Replacement of these more expensive inventories usually forces an early and sometimes sharper demand for short-term funds. Parenthetically, corporate profits appeared to rise by more than the inflation rate, delaying to some degree the need for long-term financing. Even in an inflationary environment, once hesitation over financing is over, longer-term capital requirements can be enormous, such as during the 1973-75 and 1978-81 Canadian capital boom periods.

During a period of inflation, any firm that merely maintains the nominal value of its assets incurs a real loss, while one that maintains the nominal value of its liabilities experiences a real gain. The problem is exaggerated when viewed in terms of depreciation accounting. Depreciation allowances, measured in terms of the original cost of plant and equipment, seriously understate the cost of replacing physical assets. Under the FIFO (first in, first out) accounting system, inventory capital gains are valued as they accrue, while LIFO (last in, first out) counts the inventory gains when they are realized. Under LIFO, inflation-induced gains on inventories are excluded except to the extent that firms reduce their inventory holdings. Thus under LIFO systems, inventory profits are generally overstated because of inflation.

On the other hand, there is a partial offset to the profit overstatement resulting from inflation. Although current accounting practices of non-financial corporations (because of the manner in which depreciation of inventories are treated) tend to overstate profits, other accounting practices on the balance sheet tend to understate profits. This understatement of profits arises from the higher interest rates that accompany the higher rates of inflation.

The non-financial corporations are usually net borrowers, since their financial liabilities are in excess of their financial assets. As interest rates rise, the purchasing power of both financial assets and liabilities declines, but on balance non-financial corporations gain, since the decline in the value of their liabilities exceeds the decline in the value of their assets. This gain may be viewed as a partial offset to the non-financial corporate interest payments; thus their real interest payments are smaller than the interest expense recorded by standard accounting practices.

John Bossons explored the effective tax rate implications of rising inflation in a paper presented to the Canadian Tax Foundation conference on November 24, 1981.[1] He estimated the rise in the effective corporate tax rate because of the overstatement of pre-tax corporate income. His study illustrated that the difference between the effect of tax rates as calculated against reported pre-tax income and inflation-corrected pre-tax income widened over the past two decades, indicating that inflation was imposing an even greater burden on corporate profits recently than it had in the past. Between 1966 and 1969, the average reported tax rate for the firms in his sample was 28.9 per cent, while his estimate of the true corporate tax rate based on some inflation adjustments was 31.4 per cent. By 1978-79, the nominal tax rate was 25.4 per cent and the inflation-adjusted effective tax rate was 36.4 per cent.

As Bossons noted, this unlegislated hike in corporate income taxes in fact is distributed rather arbitrarily among firms and tends to raise the relative price of capital goods in the production process in Canada. That is, inflation, with its impact on accounting and taxation practices, deters capital deepening in this country, a necessary condition for improved productivity.

The individual is by no means immune from the inflation accounting problem. The following sample calculation, as shown in Table 2-2, reveals the impact of inflation on the rate of return to personal savings.

TABLE 2-2
AFTER-TAX REAL RATE OF RETURN ASSUMING CONSTANT REAL RATE OF RETURN OF FOUR PER CENT
(%)

Rate of Inflation	(Pre-tax) Real Rate of Return	Current Interest Rate	After-tax Real Rate of Return	
			With 50% Marginal Tax	With 25% Marginal Tax
0	4	4	2.0	3.0
5	4	9	−0.5	1.75
11	4	15	−3.5	0.25
15	4	19	−5.5	−0.75

A saver who on a pre-tax basis may earn a comfortable 4 per cent real rate of return, experiences a substantial drop in his capital when inflation rises, irrespective of the market-determined real rate. Assuming the saver is in a 50 per cent marginal tax bracket, then the after-tax real yield is 2 per cent in a world of no inflation, a decline of 0.5 per cent at a 5 per cent inflation rate, and a decline of 3.5 per cent when inflation is running at 11 pert cent. Even the attractive 19.5 per cent 1981 CSB issue yielded a negative real after-tax return to savers in the 50 per cent tax bracket ([50% of 19.5]−11% = −1.25%).

Yield Instability, Risk and Interest Differentials

As interest rates rose under the pressure of inflation, rates generally were perceived to be more unstable or variable. The variability of interest rates is an acknowledged measure of risk in the marketplace. Thus higher rates of inflation have probably resulted in the incorporation of a higher risk premium into the yield structure than existed prior to 1971. Also, the higher rates of inflation have tended to alter historical norms on yield differentials. (See Table 2-1.)

Public and Private Economizing on Cash

When Canadian interest rates climbed to unprecedented heights in 1974 and considerably higher levels in 1980 and 1981, the incentives for individuals and institutions to economize on their non-interest-bearing cash and demand deposits became overwhelming. As a result, businesses and consumers are probably now keeping a larger part of their transaction and precautionary balances in interest-bearing liquid assets than prior to the 1970s. The drying up of corporate bond financing and the public shift away from demand deposits have both stemmed from increases in the general rate of inflation. But both of these behaviour changes complicate monetary policy, for it is now much more difficult to identify the most appropriate definition of the money supply. The narrowest definition of the money supply, which includes demand deposits plus currency in circulation, clearly seems the most outdated.

Conclusion

Accelerating rates of inflation over the past decade have favoured those financial institutions which were able rapidly to adjust the rates they offer on their liabilities, so as to keep up with open market interest rates. On the face of it, this appears to have increased the competitive advantage of the chartered banks vis-à-vis the trust companies, and the near banks relative to the contractual savings institutions. Partly this has stemmed from the fact that higher rates of inflation tend to induce corporations and individuals to economize more effectively on their cash balance holdings, and the public has no doubt become much more sensitive to the various alternative ways of investing its savings.

Unfortunately, most economists believe that inflation will continue as an ongoing problem for the economies of the Western world in the 1980s, and therefore that the capital markets will continue to have to adjust to the high general rates of inflation and to the greater variation of inflation that is associated with a step-up in inflation itself. That is, since a higher average rate of inflation results in a greater absolute percentage point variation (or a greater amplitude) in inflation, this effect alone tends to generate greater interest rate variability. Thus the risk premium built into nominal interest rates probably has increased because of the general increase in inflation that we have seen in the late 1970s and the early 1980s.

In essence, this chapter has attempted to identify a variety of non-neutral implications stemming from inflation on institutions and the carrying out of businesses. But there is one additional non-neutrality in the inflation process which cannot be overlooked. Inflation, which some argue is caused only by monetary policy excesses, results in tighter monetary and fiscal policies than would otherwise be the case, and through this policy response usually generates lower economic growth and higher unemployment. Moreover, when the rate of inflation in Canada is higher than in the U.S. (as it was in 1981, for example), the Canadian government, which more often than not is committed to supporting the external value of the Canadian dollar as part of its anti-inflationary posture, adopts higher interest rates in Canada to stabilize the downward pressures on the currency. Thus there is a major non-neutral effect on the economy from inflation which flows through the adoption of tighter monetary policy and the apparent weakness of the Canadian dollar as a result of inflation rate differences between Canada and the U.S.

Central Bank Monetarism and the Capital Markets

3

Central Bank Monetarism

High and volatile interest rates since the late 1970s have rendered capital market instruments in Canada more precarious for investment purposes. This conclusion was stressed in the previous chapter. Moreover, one cannot ignore that in part the unstable and high interest rate trend in Canada also correlates closely with the adoption of monetarist central banking practices in Canada and the U.S. The Canadian government and the Bank of Canada embarked on a distinctive monetarist policy direction in 1975 when the bank adopted anti-inflationary monetary aggregate growth rate targets, and at the same time stated that it would no longer be as expressly concerned with interest rate determination. Ironically, since 1978 its attention to interest rates has remained particularly keen due to its use of interest rates for supporting the external value of the Canadian dollar.[1]

Despite the fairly clear monetarist tone at the Bank of Canada, Governor Gerald K. Bouey has been very sensitive to the monetarist label.

> There does seem to be an impression around that a few years ago some of us in the Bank of Canada were struck down on the road to inflation by a blinding light — the word "blinding" is sometimes emphasized — and experienced a sudden conversion to a new far-out religion called monetarism. I have to confess that I was there at the time and that nothing quite so dramatic happened.[2]

Bouey also pointed to the exchange rate management role as a practical example of Canada's independent monetary policy. But Ottawa's exchange rate fixation has tied Canada's interest rate structure more closely to U.S. rates and has spurred accusations that the Bank of Canada is simply operating as the thirteenth Federal Reserve District of the U.S. monetary system. This charge has some

34

credibility, because the bank has aimed at shoring up a weakening Canadian dollar in this era of high world inflation and high U.S. interest rates. Considering the extraordinarily erratic interest rate movements that have emanated from the U.S. since 1979, it is not surprising that the Canadian economy, and its currency, have never seemed far away from a foreign exchange crisis since 1979.

The irony in Bouey's disclaimer of monetarist orthodoxy is that in 1975 a monetarist supporter of the bank labelled it as the most monetarist central bank in the Western world. He has since recanted these views.[3] While the bank's attention to interest rates for external exchange rate purposes represents some movement away from pure monetarism, nevertheless interest rate intervention since 1975 has generally been poised to tighten monetary conditions in Canada, seldom to ease them.

The official 1981 growth rate target ranges for monetary aggregates in Canada, 4 to 8 per cent for M1 (currency plus demand deposits at the banks), seem rather inconsistent with the 10 per cent or more average inflation rate projected for the Canadian economy until 1990 in most long-term studies. But the money supply rule continues to be an important determinant of policy making in Canada, despite its rather unsatisfactory performance with respect to moderating inflation in Canada. Purer forms of monetarism took hold in Great Britain and the U.S. when Mrs. Thatcher and Mr. Reagan took office. It is in those countries that the success or failure of the doctrine will be more decisively determined.

The American brand of monetarism, as combined with other policy actions in that country, is particularly important to Canada in terms of the generation of high nominal and real interest rates. As usual, what happens in the Canadian economy is very much dependent on what happens in the U.S. economy. As for the financial markets, it is the U.S. interest rate trend which appears to determine the trend of rates in Canada, subject to allowances for inflation rate differences and/or other special balance of payments factors.

U.S. policy is predicated on a questionable belief in the efficacy of "supply-side economics" combined with simplistic monetarism. Supply-side economics, the view that tax reductions and tax reform will provide incentives for increased capital investment and increased work effort, has very little empirical substance behind it. There is no reason to doubt that behaviour responds to incentives, but there is considerable evidence which indicates that the intended increases in production and productivity cannot occur rapidly enough to match the aggregate demand increases that follow from the administration's expansive fiscal position. In 1981 and early 1982 the financial markets and the financial press responded to the prospects of fairly high U.S. government deficits with alarm. Whether or not "Reaganomics" will prove inflationary over time is debatable, but the short-run effects are to cause unusually high "real" interest rates.[4] Nevertheless the trend rate of inflation in the U.S. is expected to average about 7 per cent per annum, or less, between 1982 and 1986, which is considerably below its recent peak of 13 per cent in 1979.[5]

Since a continuation of the strict U.S. monetarist practices seems likely, and since U.S. government borrowing requirements are expected to remain high in coming years, the aggregate demand for funds in the U.S. credit markets cannot moderate to the extent hoped for by the U.S. administration. This has increased the risk premium in interest rates to such a degree that few economists in early 1982 expect low real interest rates in the U.S., despite cyclically low inflation rates.

Further, there is also the danger that with rising deficits pushing fiscal policy in one direction and monetary policy pushing in another, the U.S. Federal Reserve will be forced to adopt even more restrictive monetary measures and/or will maintain the level of restriction far too long. In early 1982 it seemed that high interest rates could continue for a while yet, and even move higher on a temporary basis.

An extension of high real interest rates in the U.S. and Canada in the medium term suggests that the interest rate sensitive sectors of the economy may move into a more prolonged economic slump than even the recent experience suggests. That is, high real interest rates will continue to restrain the housing industry, the automobile industry and capital investment, and in the process curb general economic growth.

The two medium-term projections set out in Table 3-1 imply that Ottawa is well aware of these possibilities. The federal Department of Finance projections for the medium term, which were released with the November 1981 Canadian budget, forecast real GNP in Canada to grow by a very sluggish 2.7 per cent average between 1981 and 1987. Even though the economic environment is supposed to be heavily influenced by megaproject investments, as it turns out, real investment expenditures for non-residential construction increases by only 2.5 per cent per annum in the Department of Finance projection for that period.[6] As well, real consumer expenditures and residential construction expenditures are also expected to remain dampened over the medium term. In a similar fashion, the base case projections published by the Economic Council of Canada also cite significant areas of

TABLE 3-1
TWO MEDIUM-TERM PROJECTIONS FOR CANADA AND THE US,
1981-87
(Percentage Changes Unless Specified to the Contrary)

	1981	1982	1983	1984-87 (Average)	1981-87 (Average)
1. DEPT. OF FINANCE (November 1981)					
US					
Real GNP	2.1	1.3	2.3	3.1	2.7
CPI	10.1	8.7	8.7	7.2	8.2
Canada					
Real GNP	3.6	2.2	2.4	2.7	2.7
CPI	12.7	11.7	10.2	8.0	9.5
Productivity	0.4	0.4	0.7	0.5	0.5
Unemployment rate (%)	7.2	7.8	8.3	7.8	7.8
2. ECONOMIC COUNCIL, BASE CASE (October 1981)					
US					
Real GNP	2.7	3.1	3.5	2.9	3.0
CPI	10.4	9.7	8.6	8.5	9.0
Canada					
Real GNP	3.5	2.6	3.3	2.8	3.0
CPI	12.5	12.2	12.2	9.7	11.0
Productivity	0.4	−0.2	0.3	1.3	0.6
Unemployment rate (%)	7.1	6.4	5.3	5.3[1]	5.9

Note: [1] 1983 and 1984.

Sources: 1. Department of Finance, "The Current Economic Situation and Prospects for the Canadian Economy in the Short and Medium Term" (November 1981), pp. 16, 18, 19.
2. Economic Council of Canada, *Room for Manoeuvre,* Eighteenth Annual Review, 1981, pp. 36, 39.

economic weakness. The Department of Finance projections are more optimistic than those of the council, which foresees a continuation of the two-digit inflation trend for some time.[7]

The financial market implications stemming from these official scenarios are rather distressing. They imply continued volatility in the Canadian exchange rate and interest rates, and depending upon the particular state of the Canadian balance of payments position or upon the existing spread between Canadian and U.S. inflation rates, also imply repeated cycles of exchange rate and/or interest rate crises.

What options are available to the authorities which would provide them with some flexibility? The Economic Council suggests that Ottawa could achieve some room to manoeuvre by accepting somewhat lower interest rates (which would imply monetary aggregate growth rates towards the upper range of the bank's targets) as well as some selected tax rate reductions.[8] The council's position is that the inflation risk from lower Canadian interest rates has been exaggerated by the bank. Moreover, it is clear that the economy and the financial markets would be better served in the volatile environment of the 1980s if interest rates were at a more "normal" level relative to the domestic rate of inflation. Yet monetarist central banking principles imply continued high real interest rates, even though there may be very little inflation relief in sight over the medium term.

Reducing Canada's inflation rate seems to be the key to restoring the health of the economy and of the capital markets. If Canada's inflation rates were lower, debt instruments would lengthen in terms of their contractual maturities, and both lower interest rates and lower unemployment would follow. Furthermore, the Canadian economy would not be subject to repeated exchange rate crises and mortgage rate problems.

The adverse effects of restriction on economic growth and employment are widely known. Tight monetary policies and unusually high interest rates have also sown the seeds for further inflation and unemployment by destroying the incentive to invest in the non-energy sectors of eastern Canada. To the extent that orthodox restrictive measures can be expected to moderate inflation, a case can be made that given the same level of unemployment or excess capacity, Canada would have been better off with an easier monetary policy and a tighter fiscal policy since the mid-1970s.[9] While a significant fiscal tightening occurred as a result of the unpopular November 1981 budget, this was not followed by any quid pro quo; Canadian monetary policy still remained unnecessarily restrictive in early 1982.

Ironically, the greatest monetarist threat to the Canadian economy at this time stems from highly restrictive U.S. monetary measures and their impact on Canada's economy via the export of high U.S. interest rates. By tradition and necessity, Canada has tied its monetary policy to that of the U.S., and the U.S. Federal Reserve has been behaving irresponsibly by imposing high and erratic interest rates that are damaging economic growth and unsettling the world currency markets. In January 1982 several Western nations announced their desire to pursue lower interest rates in independence of high U.S. rates. But these countries began to experience a favourable shift in their international current account positions, which provides them with additional degrees of freedom in their monetary policies.

It would probably be advantageous for Canada if the central bank allowed the Canadian currency to fluctuate more freely (or on occasion to devalue further) rather than continuously to accept intolerably high interest rates from the U.S. The Bank of Canada seems to be attempting to stabilize the Canadian dollar somewhere above 81 cents U.S.; its 1981 low point of 80 cents U.S. made the bank uneasy. In support of the exchange rate, the bank drove the prime lending rate at the Canadian chartered banks to the unprecedented high level of 22.75 per cent in August 1981. Interest rates were much higher than was warranted at that time in terms of achieving domestic monetary growth targets, and were certainly punitively high in real terms. But during the first half of 1981 Canada experienced an unprecedentedly large capital outflow, which also tended to raise short-term interest rates.

High Real Interest Rates and the 1981-82 International Slump

In this section, the real interest rate issue is explored in more detail. As already noted, the real interest rate is a measure of the true cost of borrowed funds, or alternatively, the real return on investing in financial capital. A rough and ready way of estimating the real interest rate is simply to calculate the difference between any designated interest rate and the prevailing rate of consumer price inflation. In fact, measures of real interest rates differ depending upon the particular interest rate chosen and how price inflation is estimated. As the statistics in Table 3-2 suggest, real interest rates in the U.S., Canada and West Germany have risen to abnormally high levels in recent years, and still remain high despite the current international slump.

International comparisons of real interest rate data are not easily made because of lack of uniformity in the statistics. Within Canada, the real interest cost of funds, based on the prime lending rates offered to preferred customers by the banks, has often been either negative or close to nil. Thus when the prime lending rate at the Canadian banks reached 22.75 per cent in 1981, the associated 10 per cent real interest rate was so staggeringly high that it set the stage for the 1982 Canadian economic slump. Since consumer and business borrowing rates are usually higher than the preferred bank lending rate, the interest rate squeeze was far more pronounced than the data in Table 3-2 indicate.

The statistics in Table 3-2 show a striking correspondence between extremely high real interest rates in the U.S. and parallel real interest rates in other countries. Thus high real interest rates have become an international phenomenon.

TABLE 3-2
NOMINAL AND REAL INTERNATIONAL INTEREST RATES AT END OF YEAR/QUARTER, 1976-81[1]

	1976	1977	1978	1979	1980	1981 (3rd quarter)
United States						
money market rate (%)	5.05	5.54	7.93	11.20	13.36	17.58
% change CPI	5.0	6.7	9.0	12.7	12.5	10.9
real rate (%)	0.0	−1.2	−1.0	+1.3	+0.9	+6.7
Canada						
money market rate	8.87	7.33	8.67	11.68	12.80	20.06
% change CPI	5.9	9.2	8.6	9.5	11.1	12.6
real rate	+3.0	−1.9	+0.1	+2.2	+1.7	+7.4
West Germany						
money market rate	3.89	4.14	3.36	5.87	9.06	11.98
% change CPI	3.8	3.7	2.3	5.4	5.3	6.1
real rate	+0.1	+0.4	+1.0	+0.4	+3.7	+5.9
United Kingdom						
money market rate	11.12	7.68	8.51	12.98	15.11	13.55
% change CPI	15.0	13.2	7.9	17.3	15.3	11.2
real rate	−3.9	−5.5	+0.8	−4.4	+0.2	+2.3
Japan						
money market rate	6.98	5.68	4.36	5.86	10.93	7.25
% change CPI	9.4	6.1	3.3	5.0	7.8	4.2
real rate	−2.4	−0.4	+1.1	+0.9	+3.1	+3.0

Note: [1] The inflation rates are measured in terms of the last quarter of a year, although in 1981 only 3rd quarter data were available. The interest rates are end of period data.

Sources: The money market interest rate series is taken from International Monetary Fund, *International Financial Statistics,* vol. 34, no. 12 (December 1981), p. 43. The consumer price index data were compiled from the Federal Reserve Bank of St. Louis, *International Economic Conditions,* October 21, 1981 and September 1977.

Extraordinarily high interest rates — particularly when compared with the prevailing rate of inflation — seem to bring about the following changes in the economy:

● There is a significant shift of income from net borrowers to net lenders, although the effects are rather complicated to sort out. Small firms, farmers and families, which rely heavily on mortgage finance, tend to be hurt disproportionately as real interest rates rise or remain high. But highly-levered large corporations such as

Chrysler or Massey-Ferguson are also adversely affected in an era of high real interest rates. The tax position of the various entities also has an effect here. Households that are on balance net lenders gain as a group because of higher real interest rates. Those households holding mortgages on their property find higher mortgage rates onerous because the mortgage interest is not deductible. Firms can deduct interest costs from their corporate taxable income. In 1981 the typical rate of return on the mortgage portfolios of most banks and trust companies was about 12 per cent, well below that year's typical 18 per cent mortgage rate. Thus, until mortgage renewal time, mortgage holders as a group were ahead of the game.

- Under a prolonged high real interest rate regime one can no longer count on residential property providing a reliable hedge against inflation. Western Europe experienced some fairly high real interest rates in recent years, and in some countries residential housing prices declined by as much as 50 per cent in the late 1970s and early 1980s. In Canada high real interest rates resulted only in a levelling-off of housing prices in early 1982.

- Investment preferences shift away from real investment in plant and equipment towards less risky forms of financial investment. But once again the general equilibrium properties are complicated. This development tends to depress economic activity and to retard the growth of business capital formation which is necessary in order to obtain worthwhile productivity gains and improvements in the standard of living. The distribution of GNP tends to tilt towards consumption and away from investment. Thus in a high real interest rate environment firms and individuals tend to favour less risky, short-term financial investments over more risky, real investment expenditures. This tends to favour short-term fixed-income investments at the expense of investments in longer-term corporate and government bonds and in corporate equity.

- The financial squeeze stemming from high real interest rates tends to be less pronounced on the service-producing sectors of the economy, which usually are not so heavily levered in terms of debt compared with the resource sector and the high technology, durable goods industries.

- Exchange rate pressures are closely related to real interest rate differences between countries. The higher the level of interest rates relative to the prevailing pace of inflation within a country, the more attractive that country becomes to domestic and international investors. Thus high interest rates in Canada are a prime support for the external value of the Canadian dollar.

41

- Finally, Canada as an international debtor country, suffers a greater transfer of real resources to its creditors because of these abnormally high international real interest costs.

In conclusion, Canada and the U.S. have not experienced such high real interest rates since the Depression when nominal interest rates were low and prices were actually declining. There are a number of signs on the horizon which indicate that the 1981-82 world slump will not easily be reversed. As long as abnormally high real interest rates prevail, business and individuals will find it more worthwhile to invest in short-term financial instruments rather than in plant and equipment expenditures.

Interest Rate Variability and Recurring Interest Rate Cycles

Aside from the high real interest rate regime that was adopted in Canada as a response to more restrictive monetarist central banking practices in the U.S., nominal interest rates in North America have also become highly unstable. The unusual variability in interest rates has also contributed to the shortening in the terms of financial contracts. Interest rate variability has also forced the typical householder into becoming far more aware of interest rate cycles, since mortgage renewals could occur at vastly different mortgage rates within a short period of time.

In 1981, for example, the conventional mortgage rate in Canada rose from a low of 15.2 per cent in January to a peak of 21.5 per cent in August. By December 1981 mortgage rates had dropped back into the 17 per cent range. Interest rates were considerably lower in 1980 than in 1981, yet mortgage rates recorded a peak-trough range of about 400 basis points. Thus the chance timing of a mortgage renewal resulted in householders being either sharply ahead of the game or badly hurt in terms of monthly payments.

In this regard, volatile, high interest rates, which are part and parcel of monetarist central banking practices, have become a symbol of our economic problems. In the U.S., for example, the prime lending rate ranged between 10.75 and 21.5 per cent in 1980 and from 16.5 to 20.5 per cent in 1981. Canadian bank prime lending rates were equally unstable, with the Canadian prime rate posting variations of about six percentage points in both years.

The added problem of wide variations in interest rates in Canada can be traced to a variety of factors, but the critical focal points are this country's high rate of price inflation and the restrictive central banking practices of the U.S. Federal Reserve system and the Bank of Canada.

Canada's interest rates are usually aligned closely with U.S. rates, but the Canadian interest rate cycle became even more vulnerable to unstable U.S. interest rates in 1981 and 1982 because the inflation trend in Canada was about 3.5 percentage points higher than in the U.S.[10] and because Canada's current account deficit is huge and growing. Moreover, a takeover wave occurred in the U.S. during the first half of 1981, and capital was encouraged to leave Canada by the effect of the NEP on energy investment and the pull of opportunities in the U.S. The final link in this combination of unfortunate circumstances was the federal government's and the central bank's preoccupation with the danger of a Canadian dollar devaluation, which they argued would add to domestic inflation.

Thus, in August 1981 when capital outflows and high interest rate pressures from the U.S. were particularly acute, the Canadian dollar fell below 81 cents U.S. and Canada's prime lending rate at the chartered banks rose to its all-time peak of 22.75 per cent. At that time, Canada's inflation rate was running at about 12.5 per cent, and Canada's monetary policy was throwing the economy right back into the slump.

In the face of such restrictive monetary measures in the U.S. and Canada, Canada's cyclical expansions could only be of short duration, while the interest rate variations were rather extensive. Thus, when the U.S. economy begins to pull out of its 1981-82 slump (perhaps as early as the second or third quarter of 1982), the all too familiar collision between rapidly increasing demands for funds and restrictive monetary policy will re-emerge. Under monetarist central banking practices, interest rate movements correlate rather closely with movements in GNP — this is supported both by fact and theory. Indeed, it was the U.S. slump which pulled interest rates down in late 1981 and which permitted some strengthening in the Canadian and European currencies against the U.S. dollar at that time.

Decoupling Canadian from U.S. Interest Rates

Under the present monetary practices, Canadians face a future of either highly erratic interest rate movements or highly erratic exchange rate movements. If this assertion is correct, it is argued that exchange rate volatility is to be preferred to interest rate volatility. This calls for some decoupling of Canadian interest rates from high U.S. interest rates, since the prospect of continuing with the status quo is proving very harmful.

Decoupling Canadian interest rates from U.S. interest rates would be far easier if Canada's inflation rate was improving, and if the balance of payments position was stronger; but genuine improvements on both fronts are simply not in the cards for 1982 and 1983. Decoupling Canadian interest from the U.S. rates could be managed under a regime of rigid foreign exchange controls, but in this case the cure could be worse that the disease, especially in terms of further strains on the fragile economic and political relationships that exist between Canada and the U.S. There remains a far simpler and more straightforward policy option.

The central bank should permit wider fluctuations in the foreign exchange value of the Canadian dollar. The government and the bank have exaggerated the risk to the Canadian economy from a temporary decline in the dollar. Such a policy would have meant that the Canadian dollar would have probably declined below 80 cents U.S. in August 1981 when the heavy interest rate/balance of payments pressures emerged. But Canadian interest rates would not have had to rise above 20 per cent, which surely has been the source of much of Canada's recent economic woes.

Indeed, if the currency had fluctuated more freely in 1981, it undoubtedly would have traded at a level not all that different from its annual average U.S. level. Moreover, the total trade-weighted external value of the Canadian currency actually appreciated in 1981. It was an exaggeration to claim that a more freely floating currency would have resulted in an overall devaluation of the currency in 1981. It simply would have meant that the foreign exchange rate would have borne the brunt of unusual U.S. interest pressures, rather than the Canadian housing industry, the 500,000 families that faced mortgage renewals in 1981, etc.

Conclusion

In summary, Canada's economy has been badly hurt by erratic, high and unstable interest rates since 1979. The sharp month-to-month changes in interest rates are costly and damaging, and as bad as Canada's inflation rate is, the level of interest rates cannot be justified except with respect to exchange rate considerations. Higher than desirable interest rates became necessary in 1981 also because of large-scale capital outflows into the U.S. and elsewhere.

The paradox of Canada's monetary policy problems in 1981 and 1982 was that it was virtually impossible simultaneously to stabilize the Canadian money supply, interest rate levels, and the exchange rate. Some choices had to be made, and the Bank of Canada chose to stabilize the exchange rate and accept wide interest rate variations. In 1981 and in the early months of 1982, the recorded money supply never reached its lower permissible level; thus the money supply growth rate rule was bridged, but on the side of even tighter monetary policy. Inflationary pressures intensified in Canada in 1981 and 1982 compared with the U.S. — a relative disparity which seemed likely to remain. The 1981-82 high wave of inflation in Canada was alarming since it occurred in the midst of an international recession and against a background of highly restrictive monetary policies and a November 1981 federal government budgetary move towards restriction.

The major source of Canada's inflation over the past several years has not been excess spending or an overheated economy. If excess demands were the chief source of the problem, then the nation's inflation rate would have responded better to the record levels of restraint in 1981 and 1982. Instead there was a series of cyclical and special factors at work, including an unusually sharp reduction in labour productivity, a wage catch-up effect, fairly hefty food price hikes, and the latest energy price increases. Canada's economic policies were designed to be moderately restrictive, but at best these policies may have kept a lid on the rate of inflation. In fact, the rate of inflation rose from 10 per cent in 1980 to 12.5 per cent in 1981. This performance is clearly unsatisfactory, and under the present mix of policies Canada risks worse inflation in later years.

This analysis has turned on several critical assumptions which are elaborated below.

- The damage imposed on the economy by the policy of shoring up the Canadian dollar using high interest rates far exceeds the potential harm incurred from allowing the dollar to fluctuate more widely within a stabler Canadian interest rate environment.
- The level of interest rates in 1981 and 1982 was so far in excess of the rate of inflation that real borrowing costs were unnecessarily high.
- The inflationary effect of a devaluation must be judged over a longer period of time (such as several years) rather than in terms of the dollar's temporary level. Over time, a more stable interest rate environment would cause wider fluctuations in the Canadian dollar, but this does not mean that the average exchange rate value would be much different than under present practices.

It seems rather likely that Canadian policy makers will continue to ace interest rate and exchange rate crises in the future unless they permit the currency to fluctuate more freely. While there are risks in moving towards a more freely determined exchange rate, the inflation risk stemming from a currency devaluation has been exaggerated out of proportion and certainly appears slight when viewed against the damage that high and volatile interest rates have imposed on the economy. Indeed this writer is not in favour of an overall devaluation, and hopes that, on average, a devaluation could be avoided.

John Cornwall has argued that economists require separate theories of inflation and unemployment because these important variables seem to have a life of their own.[11] This observation seems to fit the post-1973 economic circumstances in Canada fairly well. The Canadian economy seems always poised for more inflation when provided with any type of economic stimulus, whether the stimulus originates from exports, domestic investment or expansionary fiscal or monetary measures. The asymmetry in the Cornwall thesis is that weakening aggregate demand translates primarily into output and employment losses, and has little or no impact on inflation.

While it is outside the scope of this study to consider the range of other macroeconomic instruments available to deal with the inflation-unemployment dilemma in Canada, the case for employing some version of a tax-based incomes policy seems even stronger in 1982 than it was several years ago.[12]

Energy Financing and the Megaprojects

An Overview of Megaproject Requirements

Earlier in this study it was suggested that the Canadian economy seems potentially able to generate the requisite sums of savings required for the purposes of financing the megaprojects scheduled to be constructed and to come on stream in the 1980s. The environment seems to require a substantial redirection of savings from government debt and mortgage finance towards business investment. But although the total flow of savings will be adequate, this in itself does not imply that there will not be a project-by-project, or a sector-by-sector, financing problem because of the characteristics of this wave of energy spending.

In fact, there is a considerable variation among experts concerning estimates of financing requirements. In 1977, the Department of Energy, Mines and Resources projected that the wave of energy spending would amount to about $180 billion between 1976 and 1980 at constant 1975 prices. The Toronto Dominion Bank, in a report prepared in 1979, projected the wave of energy investment to amount to $325 billion in current dollars for the period of 1978 to 1990. The Royal Bank of Canada undertook a study for the Polar Gas Project, and its energy projection amounted to a cumulative 1979-2000 figure of $1,402 billion at current prices. The Royal Bank estimate is roughly divided equally in real terms over the two decades. The Major Projects Task Force study of the inventory of projects provided a cumulative sum of current dollar expenditures amounting to $431 billion. Finally, Informetrica identified 135 major projects in a report dated April 25, 1980, and its estimates in current dollars of the total catalogue of projects amounts to $120 billion for the decade of the 1980s.[1]

These different studies indicate that not all of the major projects, whether energy oriented or not, will be concentrated in western Canada. In western Canada the inventory of potential large projects is dominated by the three major oil sands projects — Alsands, Cold Lake and Lloydminster — and the Polar Gas Project. In other words, one has to recognize that major projects on the drawing boards extend well beyond the western boundaries, even though energy projects in the West dominate the headlines.

As the statistics in Table 4-1 indicate, the Major Projects Task Force figure of $431 billion over the next two decades is dominated by electric power generation and transmission, conventional hydrocarbon exploration and development, heavy oil development, pipelines, and hydrocarbon processing and petrochemicals. The task force indicates that approximately 45 per cent of total project expenditures will occur in Alberta, British Columbia, the Yukon and the Northwest Territories, and approximately 30 per cent in the central provinces of Ontario and Quebec, while only 15 per cent of the spending will occur in the Atlantic region and in Manitoba and Saskatchewan. About 10 per cent of the task force expenditures could not be allocated to specific regions.

The calendar for prospective large-scale energy-related projects for the early 1980s is indeed rather impressive. Some dimension to the wave of investment and financing for the years 1980 to 1983 can be seen in the energy project assumptions used by John Grant in a paper on the NEP and its impact on financial markets in Canada.[2] His near-term estimates are set out in Table 4-2.

As Grant goes on to argue, government demands on the capital markets in Canada are expected to weaken during the first half of the 1980s; therefore, the first half of this decade should in theory be an appropriate time for tapping the equity and debt markets in terms of raising the large sums of money needed to finance these projects. While timing is certainly one of the key factors in terms of the operations of the market, it cannot be easily or comfortably predicted in advance — one can only make a plausible generalization as Grant has done. Indeed, in almost complete contradistinction one can make a seemingly plausible argument that the likelihood of financial "crowding-out" increases with higher inflation, tight money and high real interest rates, and these characteristics could also represent the reality of the next half decade.

Golden and Freeman commented on one aspect of financial crowding-out when they noted in 1975 that the then rapid rise of inflation created special problems for the financing of megaprojects in North America.

. . .the ravages of inflation have contributed to a rapid deterioration in

TABLE 4-1
SUMMARY OF THE MAJOR PROJECTS TASK FORCE
INVENTORY OF LARGE INVESTMENT PROJECTS TO THE YEAR 2000
($ millions)

	% of Total Expen.	Total	Multi-Prov. Unknown	Atlan-tic	PQ	Ont	Man	Sask	Alta	BC	Yukon/ NWT
Conventional hydrocarbon exploration & development	17.8	76,810	2,500	11,500				700		250	61,860
Heavy oil development	9.9	42,735						1,750	40,985		
Pipelines	7.5	32,160	27,090	935					1,660		2,475
Processing & petrochemicals	7.0	30,205		500	3,150	985		2,300	12,855	10,415	
Electrical gen. & trans.	45.7	196,855	620	29,870	66,335	38,435	10,375	3,160	18,250	29,710	100
Forest products	1.8	7,700		310	1,210	1,655			1,200	3,325	
Mining	3.7	15,825		1,010		3,900	500	3,565	1,180	5,165	505
Primary metals prod.	1.4	6,235		1,025	1,300	1,410	500			2,000	
Transportation	1.3	5,605		420	2,015	150				2,845	180
Manufacturing	2.6	11,280	8,575	400	175	1,980			145		
Defence	1.2	5,105	4,825	280						150	
Total		430,515	43,610	46,250	74,185	48,515	11,375	10,775	76,275	54,410	65,120
% of total expenditures			10.1	10.7	17.2	11.3	2.6	2.5	17.7	12.6	15.1

Source: Draft statement by the Major Projects Task Force, 1981, Table 4-1

the creditworthiness of many borrowers. This has been particularly dramatic in the public utility sector, which experienced some 36 quality downgradings in 1974 from Moody's alone or more downgradings than in any of the previous twenty years. Unfortunately, it is expected that many industrial enterprises will experience a similar fate as profits shrink and debt service grows.[3]

Clearly inflation makes financing difficult under any circumstances, and the problems of high inflation and high interest rates certainly will be compounded as they impact on the financing of some of the megaprojects described here. Part of the difficulty relates to the sheer scale of the projects considered, the fact that many of these projects have pay-off periods which are very distant in the future, as well as the fact that the public review procedures, while very necessary, also create additional delays and increase the costs and uncertainty associated with project financing.

TABLE 4-2
MAJOR ENERGY PROJECT ASSUMPTIONS
($ millions)

	1980	1981	1982	1983
Alaska Highway gas pipeline	250	590	550	1,870
Q and M pipeline	70	550	480	590
Lloydminster heavy oil extraction	90	100	100	100
Cold Lake tarsands plant	50	100	750	1,100
Alsands tarsands plant	20	50	800	1,000
SNG plant & benezene plant	20	115	125	107
Great Canadian oil sands plant expansion	95	80	—	—
Northeast BC coal project	—	100	300	400
Hibernia				
Grand Banks exploration	175	200	200	200
Development	—	—	450	600
Beaufort Sea				
Exploration	200	250	250	250
Development	—	—	400	900
Hydro Québec	2,888	2,950	3,500	3,500
Ontario Hydro	1,750	2,000	2,176	2,220

Source: John Grant, "The National Energy Program and Canadian Financial Markets," in G.C. Watkins and M.A. Walker, *Reaction: The National Energy Program* (Vancouver: The Fraser Institute, 1981), p. 132.

The sum total of all these risks and uncertainties gives the marketplace the jitters over the amount of money required and the extent of the terms to maturity. The total scale of the projects is so large that their financing structure must be more heavily based on debt rather than equity financing. In a period of high interest rates when the term to maturity of outstanding debt has shortened, the crux of the project financing problem is that the projects can rarely be expected to pay out a stream of revenue within the maximum maturity at which banks or other lending institutions are willing to provide funds.

Moreover there is a question of the similarity of risk available to Canadian lenders and the lack of availability of diversification because of this wave of energy spending. Myron J. Gordon has tackled this issue directly in a paper reviewing the costs and benefits of foreign ownership.

> Investment in a tarsands plant can be risky in many other ways, too, but the important point for us is the fact that the law of diversification makes investments much riskier for a Canadian firm than it is for a multinational corporation and its stockholders. Each of the foreign investors would be taking a piece of the tarsands plant that would be only a negligible fraction of his/her portfolio — actually reducing overall risk. On the other hand, ownership of a tarsands plant by a Canadian firm would put a large fraction of the wealth of the company and of its Canadian stockholders in one basket.[4]

It is the role of the capital markets to allocate funds efficiently among the most profitable of the investment projects subject to the acceptable risk criteria. It is also clear that part of the problem with financing megaprojects lies in the potential bunching effect upon the capital markets — which relates once again to the timing issue — and in the perceived private lender's risk, which in part depends on the uncertainty of government restrictions on ownership of project assets, and in part on the uncertain impacts of government measures on the revenue stream itself.

As Gordon indicates, the Canadianization goal of the NEP presents investors and governments with a challenge, since the key issue is more often the question of risk rather than total size of the capital markets. For example, the Canadian government, offering fairly risk-free securities, was able to finance about $12 billion of new money in 1981. The capital markets' ability to supply such funds is fairly well documented. But as the risks associated with the security financing increase, the market is less willing to supply funds. Many of these large energy projects will be undertaken in a regulated

51

environment, and for acceptable financing to occur in one way or another, some form of federal or provincial financing may be required to provide these projects with sufficient high corporate bond rating. In addition, governments could ensure an easier completion of projects if they would guarantee interested parties that the projects would be completed.

Throughout most of the postwar period the most important sources of institutional funds for large-scale projects were the life insurance companies in Canada and the U.S., which in turn were the leading institutional purchasers of bonds. However, since the late 1970s, corporate bond financing has nearly dried up in both countries, and the chartered banks in Canada and the commercial banks in the U.S. have become more important lenders in terms of their capacity to meet these large-scale requirements. It should also be remembered that life insurance companies, or indeed any institutional portfolio management firm, desire to avoid over-concentration of securities from any single project or company in their portfolio of assets. This comes back to the question of the Canadianization of the energy projects and the need to concentrate the finance in Canada.

Issues Involved in Project Planning and Financing

The financing of the huge inventory of projects described in the previous section will occur primarily under the umbrella description of "project financing."

> The essence of this type of financing involves the creation of a separate project entity which issues securities that are structured in such a way that the debt service and equity returns are provided by the revenues generated by the project. This contrasts with conventional financing in which the lender relies more on the general creditworthiness of the borrower than on the revenues from any particular project.[5]

Lenders involved in project financing face a series of long-term risks, and as a result, they usually insist that a creditworthy party or parties enter into a commitment to provide any funds over and above the original financing plan that are necessary to complete the project or to pay off the debt in the event of non-completion.

> Other risks which lenders face are that the flow of revenues from the project would be (1) interrupted by an outage or prolonged interruption of service, or (2) insufficient to keep the project operating and cover debt service. To protect against such contingencies, lenders commonly insist that users of the project's output or service enter into what are

called "take-or-pay contracts" or "all events full cost of service contracts."[6]

Under such a contract the purchaser is obligated to pay a minimum amount sufficient to service the project debt and cover certain other project costs even if he does not receive output from the project. In short, he pays regardless of what other events may occur. By not inviting foreign capital, Canadian portfolio managers are in fact invited to accept a larger risk than may be potentially warranted from the perspective of maintaining the value of their portfolios. This is why a role for government in the megaproject financing process seems an integral part of the process.

As already noted, a basic problem with many of the megaprojects is simply their overall massive scale combined with the long period of time until revenues increase sufficiently to reduce debt outstanding. That is, while projects such as a Canadian tarsands project must be large-scale in order to generate the production efficiencies necessary, nevertheless the amounts of capital financing required to support the construction expenditures and to purchase new machinery and equipment are so immense, with revenue returns so distant in the future, that it is difficult for the capital markets to become involved in the financing. Indeed, it requires a peculiar kind of financial ingenuity to shape the right financing package to match the risks lenders are willing to accept with the funds that are available.

While some of what follows may sound a bit naive, a case can be made, in view of the large number of hold-ups that occur because of financing problems, that the engineers and planners will have to develop smaller-scale projects, ones which can be more easily incremented, in order to provide the revenue flows to fit the financing plans. Otherwise, the sheer scale of these projects, such as the Foothills Alaska Highway Pipeline of $12 billion or the potential Polar Gas Project of $20 billion, seems to guarantee the necessity of a government presence. Even if the net economic and social benefits of a particular project are overwhelmingly positive, experience thus far suggests that private financing will not necessarily be available without some government guarantees or other form of intervention.

In view of these comments, any concern with the capacity of the Canadian capital markets to supply funds should be addressed more to the matching problem, the bringing together of the borrower and the appropriate pools of risk capital, than to the overall size of the capital markets.

Financial Risks Faced by Investors

Investors generally face two types of financial risks: the risk of non-completion of the project, or the risk that once the project is completed revenues will be insufficient to cover all project costs, including debt service charges. Non-completion can result from many causes, including unforeseen construction difficulties, environmental legal problems or other legal or administrative political difficulties. Insufficient revenues often arise from the failure of regulatory agencies to allow the investor to recover the full project costs or from the interruption of gas flow due to natural disaster, mechanical failure or other major events.

Thus there are essentially two questions posed when these projects reach the regulatory stage and are assessed by governments or their agencies: (1) is the carrying capacity of the financial markets themselves sufficient, and (2) is the capacity of the participants in the consortium sufficient to put together the right blended package of equity and debt so that investors will be prepared to undertake the investment risk?

As Golden and Freeman noted in a speech given several years ago, from a lender's perspective project financing comprises a three-point detailed review of:

— the facility or productive asset which will be built or developed;
— the users or customers of the facility;
— the strategic link between the facility and its users.[7]

Many of these proposed large projects provide governments with a dilemma: on the one hand, the projects in themselves seem to offer substantial net benefits to the economy, but on the other hand, even if the benefit-cost ratios are favourable, this does not necessarily mean that the projects can be viably financed in private markets. Thus governments have difficulty in sanctioning the use of public guarantees for private ventures even when they are in the national interest. The rationale for this is obvious. Governments are forced to make the right guesses about the course of a series of external events just as the private sector is, and when the private sector is unwilling to justify an investment risk, it often is just as difficult for the public sector to step in.

With this in mind, let us look at two examples of how governments have affected project financing. The first case considers the financing of the Alaska Highway Pipeline Project (AHPP), a private project which required approval by both the U.S. and Canadian national governments and regulatory agencies. The original private consortium did not request government assistance, but over time their preferences shifted because of the obvious unwillingness of the private capital markets to accept the perceived risks involved. The break-even point for projects on as large a scale as the AHPP is quite far into the future, yet the financial markets wish to avoid fixed-term commitments in excess of five years' duration. The second case study reviews the financing of an ethylene plant in Alberta and the ingenious tax and financial arrangements that were necessary for the project to be completed.

Financing the Alaska Highway Pipeline Project

In some respects the AHPP is more important to the U.S. than to Canada; and financing problems, cost escalations and government regulations — even more than the technical and engineering considerations — seem to have been the critical factors causing delays and changes in the objectives of the project.

The natural gas pipeline system, as originally proposed, was supposed to carry natural gas from Alaska's North Slope through Canada to California and into the midwestern states. The project involved Canadian governments and regulatory authorities because the 4,800-mile pipeline was to move natural gas from Prudhoe Bay across Canada and into the lower forty-eight states at a point near Calgary, Alberta. The pipeline was then expected to split into a western leg serving the U.S. coastal states and an eastern leg serving the midwestern states.

Some time ago, the U.S. Federal Energy Commission provided conditional approval for the building of the mainland U.S. segment of the pipeline even in advance of the completion of the Alaska and Canadian segments. Canada recently constructed the pre-build section of the line in southern Canada, which had the effect of extending the construction phase for the entire project well into the future.

The U.S. government specified that the project should be privately financed, and so far that decision is still in force, though it is clearly subject to change. A joint U.S.-Canadian government agreement on principles for the project also called for private financing in both the U.S. and Canada.

Since the sourcing of the gas was to have been in U.S. territory, not surprisingly the major regulatory bottlenecks were in the U.S. rather than in Canada. Some would argue that the Canadian government agreement to pre-build some of the line was a hastily and ill-conceived measure disguised to increase Canadian exports of natural gas into the U.S. market. Nevertheless, aside from the financing difficulties, U.S. decision making was hung up on (1) the mechanism by which the wellhead price for gas was to be determined, (2) the method by which gas was priced for the ultimate consumer, (3) the authorization of an efficient flow of gas by the state of Alaska, (4) negotiation of sales contracts, (5) the rate of return that governments would allow on an investment in a transportation system, (6) formation of a final consortium of equity investors in the project, and (7) a determination of the extent to which the benefiting parties (including the producers of the gas, the state of Alaska and the gas consumers) would provide financing to support the projects. The U.S. federal government has the ability to resolve a number of these issues.

In 1977, a report presented to the U.S. President suggested that roughly $9.5 billion worth of financing would have to be raised for the AHPP between 1978 and 1982, and that the capital markets of the two countries could have managed that task between them quite easily.[8] The applicant at that time intended to exploit the U.S. commercial banking system, the Canadian chartered banks, the U.S. long-term debt market and the Canadian long-term debt market. The report also concluded that there was good reason to expect that private financing could support a viable transportation system.

Indeed, even as far back as December 1975, a report to Congress on the U.S.-Canadian gas pipeline project indicated:

> The relevant capital markets (in the U.S. and Canada) should have the capacity to provide the needed funds to finance privately either of the several competing systems, provided the project is established as creditworthy and the returns offered on the investments are competitive with the returns on the alternative investments relevant for each sector of the capital market that will be tapped.[9]

But Tussing and Barlow, two well-known U.S. energy consultants hired by the state of Alaska, have argued that the project should not go ahead unless it has guaranteed U.S. government backing. They indicated in a report published in April 1979:

> The Alaska Highway gas pipeline cannot be financed and built unless the United States government guarantees at least part of the projected debt. This judgment, which the authors related in an earlier report to the Alaska legislature, is held almost unanimously by the natural gas transmission industry, Alaska gas producers, investment bankers, lending institutions, state and federal regulators, and concerned members of Congress.[10]

56

Thus, financing problems in addition to environmental concerns and overlapping jurisdictions contributed to holding up the construction of the entire project. Yet, it may well be that the financial concerns are simply proxies for burdens and battles that are important in other arenas.

As of spring 1982, the U.S. Congress had not yet approved the bill to permit private financing of the pipeline. The sponsoring pipeline companies, the Reagan administration and Canadian Pipeline Commissioner Mitchell Sharp all agreed that the project is doomed unless congressional approval comes through. Even with such approval, there is still no certainty that enough money could be raised from lending institutions around the world.

Recent cost estimates for the pipeline range from U.S. $40 billion to as much as $60 billion for a North Alaska treatment plant and the 4,800-mile line to carry the gas to U.S. markets through Canada.

Financing an Ethylene Plant in Alberta

Hugh Anderson, writing in *The Globe and Mail* on March 16, 1981, cited the ingenious packaging needed to finance an ethylene project sponsored by Alberta Gas Trunk Line Co. in 1977. The project financing ultimately involved a number of U.S. insurance companies and a consortium of Canadian banks. The following paraphrase of Anderson's column illustrates the complicated steps.

The saga began with a tax legislation change, introduced in 1975, which permitted companies to write off 50 per cent of their capital costs of new manufacturing plants against corporate income in the first year of construction. The Alberta government provided written assurance to the Alberta Gas Ethylene Company (a wholly-owned subsidiary of Alberta Gas Trunk Line Company Ltd., now Nova Corporation, Calgary), Dow Chemical of Canada Ltd., Sarnia, Ontario and Dome Petroleum Ltd., Calgary that the price of the plant's raw material — natural gas — would remain competitive.

Dow Chemical Co. of Midland, Michigan, agreed to take a fixed quantity of ethylene on a take-or-pay basis; that is, it would pay for the ethylene even if it was not getting it, in almost all circumstances. Dome Petroleum also agreed to a similar long-term contract for the ethane that would be surplus to the need of Alberta Gas Ethylene, which it could export.

Because Alberta Gas Trunk was a regulated utility, it set up a separate subsidiary to handle the project. This decision posed a tax problem. The new subsidiary would not be able to take advantage of

57

the federal government's generous write-off provisions because it would not be making an operating profit for some time.

Negotiations on a number of complicated schemes dragged on until Dow Chemical became impatient. The company also agreed to buy all of the output, which made it the ultimate financial backstop for the whole project. With this top-quality credit behind the project, the U.S. insurance companies were willing to commit long-term money at a fixed interest rate. But the tax problem remained.

The dilemma was, in effect, solved by "borrowing" the tax base of the Canadian banks. Under a system of "back-to-back" financing, the U.S. lenders handed over their money to a U.S. subsidiary of Alberta Gas Ethylene. The subsidiary deposited these funds with the Canadian banks, which simultaneously loaned an equivalent amount to Alberta Gas Ethylene in Canada by buying income debentures of the company. Ironically, the federal government removed large-scale term preferred financing by the chartered banks in the 1981 budget.

Both of these cases, the AHPP and the ethylene plant project, indicate that it is less likely that the size of the total absolute credit pool will limit investments in large projects in the 1980s, but rather than the megaproject risk allocation issue will prove the major problem. So much of investment spending in Canada is already concentrated in energy-related projects that portfolio diversification alternatives are already limited, and this suggests that the U.S. capital markets will more than likely have to be tapped for funds. This represents a fundamental public policy dilemma for a federal government committed to reducing the role of foreign investment in the economy.

Conclusion

Canadian governments and businesses have always been involved in the financing of megaprojects, but the new wave of project financing in the future is particularly heavy, and unusually centralized in Alberta. Moreover, there are overlapping government jurisdictions and regulations which are involved in the approval of many of these ventures.

This chapter provided two illustrations of the frustrations with project financing when the need for government regulation and approval is involved. But government involvement is virtually guaranteed in any case because of the large sums of money involved, the heavy risks associated with some projects which private investors would shun unless offered some type of guarantee, as well as the overriding question of public concern. The problem with large project financing is that government involvement, although necessary, tends to inhibit the attraction of private capital because it sets up a completely new level of risk for the investors. In addition to the fear that governments might change the rules of the game are the risks of regulatory delay in an inflationary, high real interest rate environment.

How does one sort out the role of the public sector in these projects? Since energy self-sufficiency represents a national public policy objective, it is obvious that the public sector must play a role in project development. Projects that exploit low-cost resources and that yield high returns obviously should be encouraged to go ahead. Projects that are primarily oriented towards export markets should rely on foreign capital and foreign risk bearing for their financing. The high-risk projects, based on expensive resources, are more questionable. Not only are the economics of these projects to be questioned, but also their massive size could mean that other worthwhile investments are squeezed out of existence.

Will the 1980s be an appropriate time in Canada's history to finance this fairly large wave of capital spending? Most long-term studies of the Canadian economy suggest that despite the huge sums that must be raised for energy financing, the supply of domestic savings should be sufficient for these purposes. But as discussed in chapters 1 and 3, there are some difficulties that surfaced in the 1970s which could continue to be around in the 1980s, particularly the drying up of the corporate bond market and the possibility of punitive high real interest rates.

Indeed the basic conclusion of this chapter is that it is not the total weight of credit demands in the 1980s which will prove difficult for the capital markets and for the economy, but rather the megaproject character of much of the capital investment spending. From the perspective of investors, portfolio diversification alternatives in Canada are very limited, particularly since most of the wave of investment, in one way or another, is tied to the energy sector. And this means that the foreign capital markets will continue to be tapped in the 1980s in a very heavy way because of these portfolio realities.

Canadianization Policies and the NEP

5

Introduction

Canada's 1980 National Energy Program (NEP) set in motion a dramatic change in the ownership and control of the Canadian petroleum industry. That policy was highly controversial, not only because the taxing schemes were designed to stimulate shifts of foreign-controlled assets into Canadian hands, but also because it set up a jurisdictional dispute between the Alberta government and the federal government over the ownership of economic rents accruing to the petroleum industry. The Ottawa-Alberta energy pricing and taxation impasse ended in late 1981, but the Canadian economy and its external balance of payments are still being affected by the policies which came into effect in October of 1980.

U.S.-Canadian economic relations were also strained in 1981 and 1982 because of the federal government's nationalist policies, although some friction would have existed even had the NEP and the Foreign Investment Review Agency (FIRA) not been in place.

This chapter considers the Canadianization impact of the NEP within the context of Canada's capital markets and balance of payments. Most economists recognize that Canadianization objectives cannot be justified solely on narrow economic criteria. Even when such attempts are made, the issue becomes a source for endless debate, and the justifications ultimately hinge on political and social factors.[1] Consequently no effort is made to justify the Canadianization program in a complete cost and benefit sense; rather this chapter addresses some of the national economic implications stemming from Canadianization transactions. Some financial data are presented in this chapter which indicate the potential flows of funds involved under a scenario of further Canadianization in the energy field. (See Tables 5-1 to 5-5.) Also, the issue of appropriate timing with respect to balance of payments policy concerns is considered. Specifically, the question is asked: Do we know enough about the medium-term consequences of Canadianization policies to worry about them? Finally, the issue of whether a Canadianization trend would occur spontaneously even if Canada's balance of payments position was fundamentally stronger is also explored.

Canadianization Transactions and the Balance of Payments

In a recent study on Canadianization and the NEP, the Bank of Montreal classified a typical takeover as occurring through three transactions.[2] The first transaction is the takeover transaction, which is recorded as a decline in direct foreign investment in Canada, that is, a capital outflow. If foreign funds are required to finance the sale, then a Canadian bank purchases U.S. dollars, and this second transaction creates a short-term capital inflow. A third and often neglected transaction occurs in the forward (or future) exchange rate market. The Canadian bank sells an equivalent amount of Canadian dollars in the forward exchange market which induces a capital market outflow from Canada. The third transaction depresses both the forward (or future) market value of the Canadian exchange rate as well as the spot rate, while Canadian interest rates also rise. The net result of all this is an outflow of foreign capital from Canada into other countries.[3]

Over the medium term, Canada's external debt and equity structure changes because of the Canadianization trend. Canadians have purchased equity — which provides ownership, control, dividends and capital gains (or losses) — and in the process they have also acquired new long-term debt, which results in future outflows of funds to service that debt. Thus in the medium term, Canadian interest rate payments to the U.S. may rise, and Canadian dividend outflows decline somewhat. The two flows of funds need not be identical; the interest outflow usually exceeds the reduction of the dividend outflow.

Depending upon the size of these future flows, Canadianization transactions can either expand or reduce future GNP. Interest and dividend receipts and payments comprise part of Canada's trade statistics and are included in the GNP calculation. Since takeovers result in a trend towards greater Canadian ownership of equity, larger interest payments flow abroad. The overall effect in the medium term is to reduce Canada's GNP unless this is matched by dividend flow reductions. The Bank of Montreal assumed that a future GNP reduction would be absorbed in the consumer sector, though this need not be the case.

It is suggested here that we really do not know all that much about

61

the medium-term effects, though the immediate balance of payments pressures are clear. As long as the takeover transaction was a fair one from the perspective of the purchaser, that is, as long as the premium paid to achieve equity control was a fair value premium, then we should probably ignore the medium-term economic effects since there are so many unknowns involved.

From a public policy perspective, Canadianization implies a repatriation of capital back into other countries, largely the United States. If the capital repatriation does not occur, then it could simply mean that one industry was Canadianized at the cost of higher foreign ownership, or control, of other industries. The crux of this effect on the capital markets would depend upon the amounts of funds involved and the time interval over which repatriation was to take place. If non-resident companies repatriate their Canadian-based assets, this would, on the surface, place some downside pressures on the external value of the Canadian exchange rate. In turn, the exchange rate moves would prompt the Bank of Canada to adopt tighter monetary conditions and higher short-term interest rates at home to stabilize the Canadian currency. For this very straightforward reason, Ottawa must continuously be aware of the capital market effects stemming from Canadianization measures, particularly the potential effects of such activities on the exchange rate and on interest rates. The exchange rate crisis in 1981 was triggered by two forces. The NEP and a merger wave in the U.S. resulted in a significant export of capital out of Canada, and the Bank of Canada continued stubbornly to support the exchange rate and tied the country's economic and political prestige to it in a very decisive way. There are also the less known medium-term effects to be considered. Supporters of Canadianization measures assume that the medium-term effects are by and large positive, although this need not necessarily be the case.

As the figures in Table 5-1 illustrate, the NEP set in motion about $6.5 billion of new acquisitions by Canadian purchasers of foreign-owned petroleum companies during the first half of 1981. Consequently, Canadian control of the petroleum industry rose dramatically in 1981.

In its 1980 *Canadian Petroleum Industry Monitoring Survey*, Energy, Mines and Resources Canada estimated that the level of foreign ownership and control of petroleum-related revenue was 74 per cent and 81.5 per cent respectively. Canadianization acquisitions reduced the level of foreign ownership by 4.5 percentage points to 69.5 per cent by mid-year 1981, and foreign control by 7.2 percentage

62

TABLE 5-1
MAJOR PETROLEUM INDUSTRY TAKEOVERS IN THE FIRST
HALF OF 1981

Company Acquired	Acquired By	Purchase Price[1] ($ m)
Petrofina Canada	Petro-Canada	1,450
Kissinger Petroleum	Ranger Oil	55
Candel Oil	Sulpetro	536
HBOG	Dome Petroleum	2,000
Alamo Petroleum Ltd.	Fairweather Gas	213[2]
Amax Petroleum Ltd.	Fairweather Gas	—
Uno-Tex	Husky Oil Ltd.	371
Union Texas of Cda	Drummond Petroleum	101
Aquitaine	CDC	1,600
Merland Explorations	Turbo Resources	132
Consolidated Nat. Gas	Merland Explorations	62
Total		6,520

Notes: [1] As reported in the press and other published sources.
[2] The $213 million figure covers the acquisition of both Alamo Petroleum Ltd. and Amax Petroleum Ltd. by Fairweather Gas.

Source: Energy, Mines and Resources Canada, *Canadian Petroleum Industry Monitoring Survey*, First Six Months 1981, p. 30.

points to 74.3 per cent. That is, each additional $1 billion of new Canadian acquisition "reduced the level of foreign ownership and control by about 0.7 and 1.1 percentage points, respectively."[4] *Monitoring Survey* data also indicate that a striking reduction has occurred in the foreign control of petroleum industry equity and assets since between 1979 and 1981. The statistics in Table 5-2 record these developments.

The Bank of Montreal estimates of acquisitions in 1981 were not all that different from the *Monitoring Survey* data. The bank study concluded that about $11 billion of takeover activity occurred during the first half of 1981, and that Canadianization activities — the purchase by a Canadian company of a foreign-owned company operating in Canada — accounted for about $9 billion over the six months reviewed. Accordingly, this wave of takeovers resulted in an additional $1.6 billion per quarter of capital leaving Canada.[5] This heightened activity weakened the Canadian dollar by 1½ cents U.S. from October 1980 to June 1981, and could cause a further exchange

TABLE 5-2
AGGREGATE ASSETS AND EQUITY OF
LARGE PETROLEUM COMPANIES OPERATING IN CANADA
($ millions)

		Dec. 1979	Dec. 1980	June 1981
Large foreign-controlled	Assets	16,020	19,554	20,529
integrated firms	Equity	8,632	11,379	12,041
Foreign-controlled seniors	Assets	6,410	8,088	8,670
	Equity	3,231	4,065	4,393
Canadian-controlled seniors	Assets	11,286	15,541	21,279
	Equity	4,001	5,361	7,036
Foreign-controlled juniors	Assets	2,611	2,358	2,472
	Equity	1,229	1,209	1,525
Canadian-controlled juniors	Assets	2,922	5,924	6,279
	Equity	1,190	1,673	1,951
Total industry	Assets	39,249	50,835	59,229
	Equity	18,282	23,687	26,673
% foreign control	Assets	63.8%	59.0%	53.4%
	Equity	71.6%	70.3%	66.3%

Source: Energy, Mines and Resources Canada, *Canadian Petroleum Industry Monitoring Survey,* 1980 and First Six Months 1981.

rate decline of 1¼ cents U.S. over the medium term simply to service the growing foreign debt. If the $1.6 billion quarterly outflow of capital continued unabated, it would eventually result in an average 5 cents U.S. devaluation of the Canadian dollar which would increase the inflation rate in Canada by about 2.5 per cent. Alternatively, if the Canadian authorities wished to hold the Canadian dollar steady, it would require a rise in Canadian interest rates (relative to U.S. rates) of about 130 basis points or 1.3 per cent. To offset the medium-term exchange rate pressures would require an additional 70 basis points hike in short-term interest rates.

It will become evident later in this chapter that the magnitude of future outflows required to support the NEP 1990 objectives are fairly modest, and that the $1.6 billion quarterly rate is far in excess of the outflows required. To stem the flow of funds abroad in 1981 which had commenced when record high interest rates prevailed in both the U.S. and Canada, Finance Minister Allan MacEachen persuaded Canadian bankers in August of that year to agree voluntarily to terminate the financing of such activities, and the takeover wave died down.

Perhaps the most striking finding in the Bank of Montreal study was its conclusion that the Canadianization wave could result in a decline in Canada's standard of living. This followed from its conclusion that larger sums of money must flow abroad over the medium term to service Canada's increased indebtedness. What is not fully recognized, however, is that the merger and acquisition wave was centred in the profitable oil and gas industry, which is expected to generate considerable economic rents to whatever group possesses ownership or control in the future. Indeed, the NEP was created in part to divert these economic rents into Canadian hands, for otherwise these revenues would flow to foreign-controlled petroleum companies which would have used these funds either to repatriate record levels of dividends or to buy up more Canadian industries.

The point is that the Canadianization trend, which began in Canada under the NEP, is designed to offer Canadian investors the potential to realize much higher capital gains and/or dividend returns than they would have in the absence of the NEP. These future capital gains were formerly unavailable, and they could stimulate overall aggregate demand and consumption in Canada to a much greater extent in the medium term.

The Timing Issue

An important background issue for government economic policy is whether there is an appropriate time frame consistent with national economic objectives for this type of capital market and exchange rate market effect to occur. Indeed, if timing is an issue, should additional government measures, fiscal incentives and/or penalties be used to promote or slow down a Canadianization trend depending on the strength of the Canadian dollar at the time?

When this study was written (1980-81) a fairly weak Canadian dollar was an important concern to the federal government, and unusually high interest rates were adopted to prop up the U.S. dollar value of the Canadian currency between 1979 and 1981. Thus, federal economic policy was faced with a conflict: encouraging the Canadianization of the petroleum industry obviously weakened the currency and encouraged the Bank of Canada to prop up the currency through higher interest rates in Canada. The federal government had other options at that time which would have allowed some insulation of Canadian interest rates from the high U.S. rates and from the defence of the dollar. These options included:

- allowing Canadian interest rates to decline — that is, accepting a more *freely* floating exchange rate would have allowed some drop in interest rates in Canada;
- even greater direct foreign exchange market intervention;
- a search for new export initiatives to support the dollar;
- foreign exchange controls and/or import controls.

The official Canadian position has consistently opposed the flexible exchange rate solution. If the Canadian dollar declined too sharply, then Canadian import costs would rise, inflationary expectations would worsen, and, it is usually argued, no one knows how far the decline could go. Moreover, a decline in the Canadian dollar would be interpreted, according to the official position, as "giving in" to inflation. Ironically, those Canadians who were opposed to the NEP on principle found additional justification for their beliefs because of high interest rates and currency weakness which they attributed to the NEP.

The key point is that when a major Canadianization effort occurred in 1981, it collided head on with balance of payments objectives and a generally weak Canadian dollar, and it resulted in a further and unwelcome tightening-up in monetary policy. To the degree that the 1981 Canadianization trend weakened the dollar, it seemed to have an unwelcome "inflationary" side-effect. Had the Bank of Canada and the government realized the speed at which Canadianization would occur in 1981, some of these problems could have been avoided by augmenting the exchange fund with borrowed funds in advance of the 1981 exchange rate/interest rate crisis.

The Empirical Dimension of Canadianization

Energy, Mines and Resources Canada noted in its 1979 *Canadian Petroleum Industry Monitoring Survey* that

> historically the foreign ownership and control of Canada's oil and gas business, reflecting the activities of foreign and especially the U.S.-based international oil companies, has been one of the highest among the industrial sectors. Participation by predominantly Canadian firms was largely confined to the highly risky exploration activity and to some sharing through farm-ins, etc., in development and production. Throughout the fifties and sixties non-residents owned nearly 80 per cent and controlled over 90 per cent of total oil and gas assets and nearly 100 per cent of assets employed in refining and marketing operations.[6]

In fact, foreign ownership and control of petroleum assets in Canada declined in the 1970s because of the growth of the public sector in the petroleum industry (Petro-Canada, the Canada Development Corporation and several provincially-owned corporations) and because of the maturation of Canadian-owned companies. The proportion of total petroleum assets under foreign ownership and control was 77.7 per cent and 89.6 per cent respectively back in 1971, but these proportions had declined to 61.5 per cent and 63.8 per cent by 1979.[7] Thus a Canadianization trend was underway in the petroleum sector even before the NEP was introduced.

According to the *Monitoring Survey*, total assets in the petroleum sector rose rapidly during the 1970s to reach $39.2 billion in 1979. With regard to the 50 per cent Canadianization target, this means that a turnover of about $4.5 billion worth of assets in ownership or $5.4 billion worth of assets in control would be required to achieve the 1990 target of 50 per cent ownership or control. In market terms, these book value figures should probably be doubled.

In another context, the Corporations and Labour Unions Return Act (CALURA) report indicated that in 1977 $92.3 billion in non-financial assets were under foreign control in Canada, while $199.3 billion in assets were in domestic hands. (See Table 5-3.) This means that 30.4 per cent of the total assets in non-financial corporations in 1977 were under foreign control and 65.3 per cent under domestic control. A further 4 per cent of total assets outstanding were not classified as under either foreign or domestic control. The equity ratios were only slightly different, as foreign subsidiaries controlled 39.6 per cent of the equity of non-financial corporations operating in Canada in 1977. (See Table 5-4.) Canadian-based control of equity amounted to 57 per cent.

TABLE 5-3
FOREIGN-CONTROLLED AND CANADIAN-CONTROLLED ASSETS—33 MAJOR INDUSTRY GROUPS IN 1977
($ millions)

Major Industry Group	Total Foreign	Total Canadian	Total[1]
Agriculture, forestry & fishing	305	—	4,063
Mining:			
Metal mining	5,127	—	13,478
Mineral fuels	10,791	7,164	17,985
Other mining	2,506	—	4,423
Total mining	18,424	17,294	35,886

TABLE 5-3 continued

Major Industry Group	Total Foreign	Total Canadian	Total[1]
Manufacturing:			
Food	2,852	4,376	7,336
Beverages	749	1,663	2,420
Tobacco products	1,020	—	1,022
Rubber products	1,353	82	1,438
Leather products	91	343	448
Textile mills	1,438	—	2,476
Knitting mills	66	—	374
Clothing industries	180	1,053	1,308
Wood industries	853	3,177	4,126
Furniture industries	146	692	903
Paper & allied industries	4,744	7,255	12,016
Printing, publishing & allied ind.	271	2,011	2,480
Primary metals	1,215	—	8,670
Metal fabricating	2,283	—	5,652
Machinery	2,395	—	3,742
Transport equipment	6,402	1,882	8,324
Electrical products	3,362	1,478	4,875
Non-metallic mineral products	2,799	—	3,998
Petroleum & coal products	12,406	—	13,442
Chemicals & chemical products	5,226	2,470	7,722
Miscellaneous manufacturing	1,263	1,215	2,642
Total manufacturing	51,113	43,063	95,414
Construction	1,905	—	16,305
Utilities:			
Transportation	3,146	20,837	24,610
Storage	45	1,082	1,152
Communication	1,968	11,634	13,630
Public utilities	873	41,351	42,270
Total utilities	6,032	74,904	81,662
Wholesale trade	7,572	19,839	28,866
Retail trade	3,221	14,328	20,494
Services	3,723	14,477	21,250
Total non-financial industries	92,296	199,321	303,940

Note: [1]Includes a small amount of unclassified assets.

Source: Statistics Canada, *Corporations and Labour Unions Return Act Report for 1977—Part I, Corporations,* January 1981.

TABLE 5-4
FOREIGN-CONTROLLED AND CANADIAN-CONTROLLED
EQUITY—33 MAJOR INDUSTRY GROUPS IN 1977
($ millions)

Major Industry Group	Total Foreign	Total Canadian	Total[1]
Agriculture, forestry & fishing	141	—	1,300
Mining:			
Metal mining	2,569	—	6,832
Mineral fuels	6,224	3,352	9,562
Other mining	1,410	—	2,211
Total mining	10,203	8,407	18,605
Manufacturing:			
Food	1,509	1,782	3,326
Beverages	355	618	977
Tobacco products	450	—	451
Rubber products	581	27	609
Leather products	47	103	153
Textile mills	609	—	986
Knitting mills	37	—	152
Clothing industries	87	398	506
Wood industries	377	993	1,385
Furniture industries	95	232	338
Paper & allied industries	2,100	3,197	5,302
Printing, publishing & allied ind.	151	928	1,131
Primary metals	739	—	4,084
Metal fabricating	1,204	—	2,459
Machinery	1,179	—	1,614
Transport equipment	3,161	656	3,820
Electrical products	1,813	750	2,566
Non-metallic mineral products	1,292	—	1,770
Petroleum & coal products	6,499	—	6,956
Chemicals & chemical products	2,599	478	3,082
Miscellaneous manufacturing	646	371	1,051
Total manufacturing:	25,528	16,905	42,717
Construction	492	—	3,998
Utilities:			
Transportation	1,133	6,731	8,013
Storage	7	317	331
Communication	603	4,090	4,695
Public utilities	443	8,905	9,367
Total utilities	2,186	20,044	22,406
Wholesale trade	2,311	6,066	8,806

TABLE 5-4 continued

Major Industry Group	Total Foreign	Total Canadian	Total[1]
Retail trade	1,418	4,626	6,904
Services	1,435	3,566	5,836
Total non-financial industries	43,714	63,551	110,573

Note: [1]Includes a small amount of unclassified equity.

Source: Statistics Canada, *Corporations and Labour Unions Return Act Report for 1977—Part I, Corporations,* January 1981.

Once again these statistics are cited to provide a crude benchmark for the question of repatriation and its impact on the Canadian capital markets.

These book value measures seriously understate asset values in terms of present market prices, since these statistics were originally derived from industry balance sheets at original or historical costs. It is fairly certain that the market value of today's assets, or equity, ranges from two to four times the historical cost data cited here.

In addition, one cannot easily determine from these aggregate statistics the amount of assets or equity that must change ownership in order to substantially lower the foreign control ratio.[8] First of all, CALURA data covers firms which have assets in excess of $250,000 or sales greater than $500,000.

> In the absence of conclusive evidence to the contrary, a corporation is considered to be foreign controlled if 50% or more of its voting rights are known to be held outside Canada or are held by one or more Canadian corporations that are themselves foreign controlled.[9]

That definition becomes even more complicated when one wants to identify the country of control, since this requires tracing the ownership links to the first parent corporation which is a resident of a foreign country.[10]

The CALURA definitions of assets and equity are fairly straightforward. Assets include cash, marketable securities, accounts receivable, inventory, fixed assets, investment in affiliated corporations and other assets. Equity represents shareholders' interest in net assets of the corporation and generally includes the total amount of all issued and paid up share capital and earnings retained in the business and other surplus accounts such as contributed and capital surplus.

If a NEP-style program was extended to the Canadian manufacturing sector, the sums of money involved would be quite enormous. In 1977, the total book value of manufacturing assets was about $95.4 billion, of which $51.1 billion, or 53.6 per cent, was under foreign control. The book value of manufacturing equity, where control resides, is considerably lower, with total equity amounting to $42.7 billion and the foreign control representing $16.9 billion, or 39.6 per cent, of total equity. If the manufacturing sector was singled out in the way that the petroleum industry was, the sums involved — when placed in the context of balance of payments investment flows — would seem extensive. That is, assuming the foreign equity ownership statistics are underestimates, and assuming a weak currency situation, it would seem neither economically feasible nor politically practical to encourage further large-scale repatriation of funds. This is especially the case when the Canadian economy is so wracked with inflation that a further devaluation of the currency would have unwelcome effects. Nevertheless, a case can be made for selective "key" industry asset conversions such as in the petroleum industry, especially when a large number of managerial and technically competent individuals already exist.

Lukin Robinson noted at a conference in January 1981 that the Canadian ownership objectives require both expansion within the Canadianized sector as well as future Canadianization takeovers.

> Financing Canadianization involves not only the acquisition of presently foreign-owned firms, but also requires that a high and rising percentage of new investment during the decade is in Canadian-owned firms, privately, as well as government owned.[11]

In this respect it is interesting to consider the possibility of achieving the 1990 NEP objectives for the petroleum sector. Industry analysts believe that it would require a further switch of about $12 billion of equity control to reach the NEP 50 per cent objective by 1990. Even without any additional switching in the ownership ratios, the Canadian percentage of petroleum revenues generated is expected to increase by from 4 to 6 per cent by 1990. Since 1 per cent of the total upstream revenue flows costs about $1 billion according to the *Monitoring Survey*, and since about 66 per cent of the revenue stream was foreign controlled in 1982, it would require an ownership shift of about 10 per cent to 12 per cent of the revenue stream, roughly $12 billion, in order to achieve the 1990 Canadianization target. Indeed, the combined market value of the shares of five large multinational oil companies

TABLE 5-5
MARKET AND APPRAISED NET ASSET VALUES OF FIVE LARGE
MULTINATIONAL OIL COMPANIES IN CANADA

	Market Value[1] ($ millions)	Appraised Net Asset Value	% Difference
B.P. Canada Ltd.	491.2	1,050.0	47
Gulf Canada Ltd.	3,213.4	6,825.0	47
Imperial Oil Ltd.	3,395.0	7,065.0	48
Shell Canada Ltd.	1,717.6	4,010.0	43
Texaco Canada Inc.	3,165.8	5,430.0	58

Note: [1]As at February 12, 1982.

Source: G.M. Notman, Research Securities of Canada Ltd., February 12, 1982.

operating in Canada amounted to about $12 billion in February 1982. (See Table 5-5.) This magnitude certainly sounds manageable, especially if the activities are spread out over the next eight years.

Could a Greater Degree of Canadianization Occur Spontaneously?

The answer to this question depends upon the localization of large pools of capital willing to shift into the Canadian equity market. The reality is that when such capital pools exist, they are under no compulsion to invest in Canada, and aside from an interest in the Canadian resource industries, most large pools of Canadian capital (excluding the captive pension funds) are as likely to invest abroad, or in the U.S., as in Canada. Ironically, the shift of Canadian investment into the U.S. in 1981 was making Canadian investment in parts of the U.S. as unwelcome as U.S. investment has become with some groups in Canada.[12] The international diversification of investment is natural and responds to essentially the same type of forces that attract capital to any region, or industry, that offers profitable economic returns.

If the Canadian economy were able to run a large balance of payment surplus, then a Canadianization trend would appear more manageable in terms of living with the expected exchange rate or interest rate pressures. That is, if it was judged that the Canadian dollar was overvalued with respect to its appropriate level for maintaining the competitiveness of Canadian industry, then the tax incentives and/or subsidies designed to spur even further Canadianization of industry would, coincidentally, place downside pressures on the Canadian dollar. In such an instance, the costs to the federal government of any

72

further Canadianization incentives would be partially recaptured through improved economic growth, reduced unemployment and improved tax revenues.

As to the issue of whether a greater degree of Canadianization would occur spontaneously if Canada's current account moved decisively in the surplus direction, that answer is unclear. If the current account were stronger, the high "net" outflows of interest and dividends would become less burdensome. But if, for example, the balance of payments position improved because of an improved merchandise trade balance, such earnings gains would be shared by both Canadian-controlled and non-resident-controlled firms operating in Canada. The earnings of non-resident-controlled firms could be used to expand their Canadian activities, or they could be repatriated to their head offices abroad.

The main point is that a current account surplus on its own provides no guarantee that the desired shift or exchange of equity ownership would occur. Indeed, a Canadianization program could occur simply by having non-residents exchange their Canadian equity for Canadian debt, no matter what position the balance of payments was in.

While an overall current account surplus is a necessary condition for increasing the degree of Canadian ownership (since it implies the economy is in a position to export financial capital), it simply is not a sufficient condition for any further Canadianization. The additional earnings of the Canadian-based and Canadian-controlled companies need not be invested at home — they could flow abroad as investments, or into the imports of machinery and equipment.

Indeed, a key industry can be Canadianized (e.g., the petroleum industry) even without a current account surplus, though as the 1981 experience indicates, the exchange rate pressures could be in an undesired direction.

In conclusion, a spontaneous Canadianization trend will likely not emerge even under the most favourable of balance of payments scenarios. If further Canadianization is desired, it will have to be propelled through the public sector — either through federal or provincial initiatives — much as it has been already under the changed taxation and ownership policies in the petroleum sector.

Conclusion
Accelerated Canadianization can only occur on a large-scale basis if the macroeconomic house is in better order. Indeed, it is highly unlikely that the federal government would desire to extend the tax

and/or other Canadianization programs, such as were introduced under the NEP, into other fields when the currency is basically so weak.

Unless Canada's inflation problem is solved and the macroeconomic circumstances improve significantly, in an era of stagflation and government monetarism, high interest rates could trend even higher and the Canadian dollar could be subject to even further discounts from current levels. All of this could result in higher import inflation and an even more precipitous decline in the external value of the Canadian dollar. This is why an extension of the Canadianization initiative beyond the petroleum industry presently carries with it significant macroeconomic and currency risk.

Canadian options in this direction would sharply improve if Canada's current account were to swing massively in the surplus direction. If that swing carried with it a large-scale appreciation of the external value of the Canadian dollar, then the timing would be ideal for further Canadianization and a repatriation of foreign capital. There is no guarantee, however, even with a substantial improvement in the current account, that a further repatriation of foreign-owned equity capital would occur.

An improved current account position provides the economy with the potential for reducing Canada's net foreign debt, and for increasing the Canadian ownership and control of investment in Canada. If policy makers and Canadians generally desire non-residents to sell off their Canadian assets, such transactions would support domestic production and employment most appropriately when the current account was in a strong, and surplus, position.

A Petro-Currency Possibility for Canada

In the view of this writer, the federal and provincial governments should consider what actions or incentives should be taken in the event that a favourable energy self-sufficiency situation actually develops in Canada. Such an occurrence is not completely inconceivable, and it could cause a petro-currency image to develop which could significantly raise the international value of the Canadian dollar. In such circumstances, a major Canadianization thrust and a repatriation of foreign equity would be directly consistent with the macroeconomic objectives of reducing upside pressures on the currency and stimulating the economy.

As to the financial flows involved with respect to the NEP's 1990 Canadianization target, the rough calculations set out in this chapter suggest that under the NEP umbrella there should be little difficulty for

Canadian firms (including Petro-Canada) in finding the resources for increasing Canadian ownership in the petroleum sector. The risks only surface when capital leaves Canada as the result of these measures.

A related question is whether Canada can afford to go it alone in the petroleum industry to a much larger degree in the future than it has in the past. This question can only be comfortably answered when the longer-term results are in from the NEP venture. The answer is probably yes, but one has to face up to the risk the country faces in terms of loss of entrepreneurship and the potential negative feedback on investment in this country. The projections referred to in this study suggest that Canada will still need to import substantial sums of foreign investment over the medium term. Aside from the macroeconomic dimension, there is the issue of whether sufficient "seed" money will be available within the private sector if the degree of Canadian ownership changes significantly, or alternatively, if the flow of foreign capital dries up.

The Westward Shift of Finance and Industry

6

Introduction

Thus far Canada's capital markets have been evaluated primarily from a national and international perspective. However, within Canada there is a concern over whether or not the capital markets are operating efficiently, especially in view of the latest pull of economic resources into western Canada. This latest concern has emerged with the realization that Canada is now experiencing its own equivalent of interregional funds recycling which in some ways resembles the fund recycling that has become identified with the OPEC countries.[1]

The international funds recycling concern has often been based either on a scenario of bizarre international political intrigue, or on the vulnerable liquidity position of the banks and/or governments of the industrial countries which hold large sums of OPEC short-term deposits. In fact neither of these international financial concerns — over a massive withdrawal of funds from the banks and over the term mismatch between their international assets and liabilities — seems to have a domestic parallel within the Canadian financial markets and the Canadian banking system. The domestic equivalent of an international exchange crisis seems even more unlikely because of the national banking structure in this country. Rather, the issue seems more generally related to questions about purchasing power shifts, shifts in provincial governments' fiscal positions, and changes in the economic and political power structure.

As Richard Simeon notes in an article in *Canadian Public Policy*:

> The conflict between producing and consuming regions, on the one hand, and between federal and provincial governments on the other, first became prominent in the early 1970's. It has been renewed more sharply by the recent round of further increases, as the regional imbalances increase and the interregional fiscal flows grow larger. . . .
> The conflict illustrates an important dimension of Canadian political

economy. Economic forces like the energy crisis have a highly differential impact. Because the domestic economy is so regionalized this impact sharpens internal divisions. Similarly, the conflict illustrates the interplay between regional interests and institutions of federalism.[2]

These regional economic and political conflicts and problems are the subject of this chapter, particularly in terms of their impact on the capital markets.

Interregional Economic Developments in the 1970s

Canada's population base has always been heavily concentrated in the two central provinces of Quebec and Ontario. The industrial base in Canada is also rather unevenly spread across the country, with the western provinces relying disproportionately on resource production relative to their sparse populations, while the two populous central provinces of Quebec and Ontario, in particular, rely heavily on manufacturing activity. Canada's manufacturing sector is widely regarded as underdeveloped compared with manufacturing industries in the U.S., Western Europe and Japan.

Since the 1970s, the world-wide recessionary conditions and the terms of trade shifts have contributed to much slower economic growth rates in the eastern provinces, while the three westernmost provinces have experienced a prolonged boom. The production of services tends to cluster closely around large population centres; consequently, most of the head offices of the service industries, including the powerful chartered banks, have been centred in Toronto and Montreal. But since the separatist Parti Québécois victory in 1976 in Quebec, a number of head offices of large firms have moved out of Montreal, primarily into Ontario and particularly into Toronto. The exodus began when the political and economic environment facing non-francophone business in Montreal suddenly turned inhospitable. Moreover business faces higher tax rates in Quebec, and Quebec's restrictive language laws on large businesses were also a contributing factor. Despite all of this, the *Toronto Star* of August 2, 1981 noted that "Montreal still has more than 60 of the 300 national head offices of major corporations in Canada but the days when a major corporation like Canadian Pacific Limited or Bell Canada Limited operated from Montreal are over."

At this point it might be helpful to review some data set out in Tables 6-1 and 6-2 on Interprovincial Migration Patterns. During the 1970s the net out-migration of people from Quebec to other provinces accelerated, and during the four years 1976 to 1980 Quebec lost 133,000 people on a net basis to other provinces, while Ontario lost

TABLE 6-1
CANADA: INTERPROVINCIAL MIGRATION, 1961-80

Prov.	Period[1]	In-Mig.	Out-Mig.	Gross Mig. (3) + (4)	Net Mig. (3) − (4)	Ratio Per 1,000 Population[2] Gross Mig.	Net Mig.	Ratio: Net Mig. to Gross Mig. (6) ÷ (5)
(1)	(2)	(3)	(4)	(5)	(6)	(7)	(8)	(9)
Nfld	1961-66	32,759	47,972	80,731	−15,213	33.6	−6.3	−18.8
	1966-71	43,582	62,926	106,508	−19,344	41.7	−7.6	−18.2
	1971-76	61,375	63,232	124,606	−1,857	46.2	−0.7	−1.5
	1976-80	42,098	48,996	91,094	−6,898	40.0	−3.0	−7.5
PEI	1961-66	18,191	21,161	39,351	−2,970	72.2	−5.5	−7.6
	1966-71	18,783	21,545	40,328	−2,763	72.7	−5.0	−6.9
	1971-76	23,206	19,452	42,658	3,754	74.4	6.6	8.9
	1976-80	17,802	15,538	33,340	2,264	68.3	4.6	6.7
NS	1961-66	104,924	132,048	236,972	−27,125	63.0	−7.2	−11.4
	1966-71	115,862	132,257	248,119	−16,396	64.4	−4.3	−6.7
	1971-76	125,355	114,047	239,403	11,308	59.2	2.8	4.7
	1976-80	91,318	90,189	181,507	1,129	53.9	0.3	0.6
NB	1961-66	88,591	114,270	202,862	−25,679	66.6	−8.4	−12.6
	1966-71	95,822	115,420	211,242	−19,598	67.4	−6.3	−9.3
	1971-76	109,878	93,079	202,957	16,799	62.3	5.2	8.3
	1976-80	78,826	72,558	151,384	6,268	54.5	2.3	4.2
PQ	1961-66	218,543	238,402	456,945	−19,860	16.5	−0.7	−4.3
	1966-71	195,124	317,859	512,982	−122,735	17.2	−4.1	−23.9
	1971-76	185,927	263,536	449,463	−77,609	14.7	−2.5	−17.3
	1976-80	108,753	242,056	350,809	−133,303	14.0	−5.3	−38.0

Ont	1961-66	468,174	382,805	850,980	85,369	25.9	2.6	10.0
	1966-71	574,248	423,536	997,783	150,712	27.2	4.1	15.1
	1971-76	476,052	514,612	990,664	−38,560	24.8	−1.0	−3.9
	1976-80	384,312	409,883	794,195	−25,571	23.5	−0.8	−3.2
Man	1961-66	132,645	156,116	288,761	−23,470	60.5	−4.9	−8.1
	1966-71	141,295	181,985	323,280	−40,690	66.3	−8.3	−12.6
	1971-76	145,198	172,025	317,225	−26,827	63.3	−5.4	−8.5
	1976-80	100,165	138,327	238,482	−38,162	57.7	−9.2	−16.0
Sask	1961-66	113,749	155,843	269,593	−42,094	57.6	−9.0	−15.6
	1966-71	114,550	195,948	310,497	−81,398	64.8	−17.0	−26.2
	1971-76	126,671	167,423	294,094	−40,752	65.4	−9.1	−13.9
	1976-80	111,479	101,386	212,865	10,093	56.1	2.7	4.7
Alta	1961-66	230,063	232,047	462,110	−1,984	65.1	−0.3	−0.4
	1966-71	289,452	257,446	546,898	32,006	70.8	4.1	5.9
	1971-76	352,105	293,535	645,640	58,570	75.6	6.9	9.1
	1976-80	370,524	258,128	628,652	112,396	80.4	14.4	17.9
BC	1961-66	262,345	184,597	446,942	77,747	51.7	9.0	17.4
	1966-71	356,868	241,903	598,772	114,965	58.6	11.0	19.2
	1971-76	377,217	284,933	662,150	92,285	56.4	7.9	13.9
	1976-80	287,641	210,323	497,964	77,318	49.2	7.6	15.5
Yukon/NWT	1961-66	18,354	23,076	41,430	−4,721	202.1	−23.0	−11.4
	1966-71	26,325	21,084	47,410	5,241	201.7	22.3	11.1
	1971-76	33,017	30,127	63,144	2,889	210.8	9.6	4.6
	1976-80	24,288	29,822	54,110	−5,534	205.5	−21.1	−10.2

Notes: [1] June 1-May 31.
[2] Population at mid-point of period, at annual rates.

Source: Statistics Canada, Cat. No. 91-208.

TABLE 6-2
ONTARIO: ORIGIN AND DESTINATION OF INTERPROVINCIAL MIGRANTS, 1961-80

Prov.	Destination	Number of Migrants				
		1961-66	1966-71	1971-76	1976-80[1]	1961-80
Nfld	From	24,258	38,027	31,713	20,868	114,866
	To	11,686	21,576	35,572	22,261	91,095
	Net (N)	12,572	16,451	-3,859	-1,393	23,771
	Gross (G)	35,944	59,603	67,285	43,129	205,961
	Ratio: N/G	35.0%	27.6%	-5.7%	-3.2%	11.5%
PEI	From	8,239	8,185	6,478	4,281	27,183
	To	5,274	6,794	9,111	6,262	27,441
	Net (N)	2,965	1,391	-2,633	-1,981	-258
	Gross (G)	13,513	14,979	15,589	10,543	54,624
	Ratio: N/G	21.9%	9.3%	-16.9%	-18.8%	-0.5%
NS	From	63,354	65,006	47,446	33,345	209,151
	To	39,718	49,669	56,672	37,436	183,495
	Net (N)	23,636	15,337	-9,226	-4,091	25,656
	Gross (G)	103,072	114,675	104,118	70,781	392,646
	Ratio: N/G	22.9%	13.4%	-8.9%	-5.8%	6.5%
NB	From	47,653	51,229	33,540	24,664	157,086
	To	30,630	36,837	44,788	29,592	141,847
	Net (N)	17,023	14,392	-11,248	-4,928	15,239
	Gross (G)	78,283	88,066	78,328	54,256	298,933
	Ratio: N/G	21.8%	16.3%	-14.4%	-9.1%	5.1%
PQ	From	157,267	213,605	168,396	153,237	692,505
	To	134,782	117,060	121,458	68,290	441,590
	Net (N)	22,485	96,545	46,938	84,947	250,915
	Gross (G)	292,049	330,665	289,854	221,527	1,134,095
	Ratio: N/G	7.7%	29.2%	16.2%	38.3%	22.1%
Man	From	51,875	54,512	47,031	32,752	186,170
	To	45,580	41,220	48,119	34,033	168,952
	Net (N)	6,295	13,292	-1,088	-1,281	17,218
	Gross (G)	97,455	95,732	95,150	66,785	355,122
	Ratio: N/G	6.5%	13.9%	-1.1%	-1.9%	4.8%
Sask	From	21,441	25,110	18,904	12,359	77,814
	To	17,834	17,588	17,248	18,776	71,446
	Net (N)	3,607	7,522	1,656	-6,417	6,368
	Gross (G)	39,275	42,698	36,152	31,135	149,260
	Ratio: N/G	9.2%	17.6%	4.6%	-20.6%	4.3%

TABLE 6-2 continued

Prov.	Destination	Number of Migrants				
		1961-66	1966-71	1971-76	1976-80[1]	1961-80
Alta	From	44,392	47,894	51,059	52,992	196,337
	To	40,049	49,339	75,536	110,299	275,223
	Net (N)	4,343	−1,445	−24,477	−57,307	−78,886
	Gross (G)	84,441	97,233	126,595	163,291	471,560
	Ratio: N/G	5.1%	−1.5%	−19.3%	−35.1%	−16.7%
BC	From	44,941	67,408	68,534	46,830	227,713
	To	54,262	80,764	102,178	79,043	316,247
	Net (N)	−9,321	−13,356	−33,644	−32,213	−88,534
	Gross (G)	99,203	48,172	170,712	125,873	543,960
	Ratio: N/G	−9.4%	−9.0%	−19.7%	−25.6%	−16.3%
Yukon/ NWT	From	4,755	3,272	2,951	2,984	13,962
	To	2,991	2,689	3,929	3,891	13,500
	Net (N)	1,764	583	−978	−907	462
	Gross (G)	7,746	5,961	6,880	6,875	27,462
	Ratio: N/G	22.8%	9.8%	−14.2%	−13.1%	1.7%
Total	From other provinces	468,175	574,248	476,052	384,312	1,902,787
	To other provinces	382,806	423,536	514,611	409,883	1,730,836
	Net (N)	85,369	150,712	−38,559	−25,571	171,951
	Gross (G)	850,981	997,784	990,663	794,195	3,633,623
	Ratio: N/G	10.0%	15.1%	−3.9%	−3.2%	4.7%

Note: [1] Four years only.

Source: Statistics Canada, Cat. No. 91-208.

26,000. The movement of Canadians into the western provinces took off sharply in the last decade, as British Columbia and Alberta each attracted about 170,000 people from other provinces, while Saskatchewan reversed its usual out-migration pattern after the middle of the last decade, and in fact attracted a net increase of 10,000 people between 1976 and 1979.

On a bilateral basis it is helpful to consider where the Ontario migrants settled. According to the Statistics Canada data set out in Table 6-2, between 1976 and 1980, on a net basis, 32,000 people moved to British Columbia, 57,000 to Alberta, and 6,500 to Saskatchewan. Ontario also experienced a small net outflow of people to other provinces, though on a net basis it attracted nearly 85,000 people from Quebec between 1976 and 1980.

The out-migration of people and capital from Quebec and Ontario is probably also a reflection of the weakness of the manufacturing industries which have been generally in the doldrums because of recessionary conditions and high interest rates. In the case of Quebec, that province relies disproportionately on such low-productivity, protected industries as shoes and textiles. These industries do not attract new investment because it is widely realized that they are not very competitive.

Regional incomes in the three westernmost provinces have also soared relative to the rest of the country over the past decade. Indeed the per capita personal income levels in Alberta and British Columbia are now the highest in the country (in excess of $12,500 in 1980) and higher than Ontario's per capita income level of $12,000. Income per head in British Columbia and Alberta are more than 50 per cent higher than in the Atlantic provinces and about 20 per cent higher than in Quebec.[3]

As Anthony Scott has noted, economists generally argue that capital is mobile if given the opportunity to shift. "Economists at least are convinced that the owners of capital, whether they be persons holding liquid securities and equities or firms holding plant and equipment, are quite ruthless in shifting wherever their net return, after taxes and risk has been allowed for, is the greatest. And experience has shown that this hypothesis can give good predictions . . ."[4]

In fact, Scott's quotation is particularly appropriate in terms of Canada's current internal movements of capital and labour. People and capital are attracted to the western provinces primarily because the economic prospects are far brighter in those regions than they are in eastern Canada.

The Regional Impacts of Higher Energy Prices

The origins of the Canadian version of the international energy crisis and the domestic funds recycling concern can be seen in Tables 6-3 to 6-5 which highlight the relative price swings between basic commodities and manufacturing goods that have occurred over the past decade. As is virtually always the case, the main thrust behind these relative price swings originated in the international markets, and the most notable feature of these price movements was the massive swings between the price of petroleum products and manufactured goods. These terms of trade changes account for the improvement in the

TABLE 6-3
PRICE OF A BARREL OF CRUDE OIL LANDED IN MONTREAL

Year	Imported Price (OPEC)			Domestic Price (Cdn $)		
	Average Wellhead (US $)	Montreal Price US $	Cdn $	Average Wellhead	Montreal Price	Subsidy (Cdn $)
1973	3.20	4.00	4.00	3.50	3.95	0.05
1974	10.85	11.30	11.05	5.80	6.30	4.75
1975	11.00	12.25	12.45	7.25	7.75	4.70
1976	11.50	13.00	12.80	8.55	9.05	3.75
1977	12.40	14.00	14.90	10.25	10.75	4.15
1978	12.70	14.15	16.15	12.25	12.80	3.35
1979	18.10	19.54	22.88	13.25	13.60	9.28
1980	29.70	31.70	37.10	15.58	16.20	20.90
1981 May	34.61	36.55	43.48	17.75	18.65	24.83

Source: Grahame H. Notman, Research Securities of Canada Ltd. (Unpublished paper, August 1981).

economic prospects of the three westernmost provinces, which have quite a stake in the petroleum industry and in all other basic commodities. As already noted, the economic prospects of the provinces of Quebec and Ontario are much more heavily oriented towards manufacturing.

The crux of this massive terms of trade shift to the western provinces began with the OPEC countries exerting their market power rather dramatically in 1974 and once again in 1978 and 1979. For example, the statistics in Table 6-3 illustrate that the average cost of OPEC crude oil rose in U.S. dollars from $3.20 per barrel back in 1973 to $34.61 per barrel by May 1981. This converts to an average cost, expressed in Canadian currency, of about $43.48 per barrel in Montreal when transportation costs are included. The equivalent Montreal price of domestic crude was about $18.65 per barrel in May 1981 and the resulting federal subsidy on imported oil amounted to $24.83 per barrel.

As the statistics in Table 6-4 indicate, between 1971 and May 1981 the price of imported crude oil rose 1,770 per cent, while the cost of domestically-produced crude was allowed to rise 540 per cent. Over that same ten years, manufacturing prices in Canada rose just under 270 per cent. The prices of other basic commodities, such as grain, coal, newsprint and lumber, all rose in excess of manufacturing price

TABLE 6-4
MANUFACTURED AND RESOURCE COMMODITY PRICES, 1960-81
(1971=100)

Year	Total Mfg Selling Price Index	Grain Price Index	Potash	Coal	Import Price of Oil	Av. Oil Wellhead Price Index	Av. Natural Gas Wellhead/ Plant Gate Price Index	Newsprint for Export (BC)	Lumber Hemlock (BC)
1960	82.2	93.5	—	102.7		83.3	65.3		
1961	82.4	99.1	—	102.1		83.7	78.2		
1962	83.3	109.8	—	101.8		83.0	82.3		
1963	84.4	109.4	106.4	102.9		87.3	88.4		
1964	85.1	112.4	107.6	97.4		88.8	94.6		
1965	86.2	108.2	113.3	99.2		89.1	93.1		
1966	88.7	115.0	93.3	110.9		89.1	98.0		
1967	90.4	114.5	83.8	76.8		89.1	98.6		
1968	92.3	109.3	66.1	74.4		89.1	98.6		107.9
1969	95.8	104.2	58.9	71.8		89.1	97.3		110.7
1970	98.1	100.7	94.2	78.5		90.6	101.4		88.5
1971	100.0	100.0	100.0	100.0	100.0	100.0	100.0	100.0	100.0
1972	104.4	116.2	104.3	110.2	109.5	100.4	104.1	102.9	126.6
1973	116.1	208.0	106.8	120.7	129.8	123.9	115.0	108.4	173.6
1974	138.1	290.0	143.8	194.9	411.3	207.2	181.6	134.7	161.7
1975	153.7	266.9	206.3	319.1	500.4	260.5	369.4	180.3	158.8
1976	161.6	232.5	183.2	327.6	525.7	304.0	600.0	180.4	173.5
1977	174.3	207.2	188.5		606.3	365.9	793.9	200.4	204.0
1978	190.4	200.2			657.2	437.3		223.5	229.5
1979	217.9	282.5			931.1	473.0		253.7	
1980	247.0	337.3			1,509.8	474.2		300.7	
1981 May	267.8	364.7			1,769.9	540.2		351.1	

Sources: Table II-8, updated by author, in Kenneth H. Norrie and Michael B. Percy, ''Westward Shift and Interregional Adjustment: A Preliminary Assessment,'' Economic Council of Canada Discussion Paper No. 201 (May 1981). Grain and newsprint prices were updated using International Monetary Fund. *International Financial Statistics*, vol. 34, no. 6 (June, 1981), pp. 104-105, while the oil prices were updated from a series

TABLE 6-5
TERMS OF TRADE BETWEEN SELECTED PRIMARY PRICES AND MANUFACTURED GOODS
(1971=100)

Year	Grain/ Mfg	Newsprint/ Mfg	Domestic Well-head Oil Price Index/ Mfg	Import Price of Oil/ Mfg
1960	113.7		101.3	
1961	120.3		101.6	
1962	131.8		99.6	
1963	129.6		103.4	
1964	132.1		104.3	
1965	125.5		103.4	
1966	129.7		100.5	
1967	126.7		98.6	
1968	118.4		96.5	
1969	108.8		93.0	
1970	102.7		92.4	
1971	100.0	100.0	100.0	100.0
1972	111.3	98.6	96.2	104.9
1973	179.2	93.4	106.7	111.9
1974	210.0	97.5	150.0	297.8
1975	173.6	117.3	169.5	325.6
1976	143.9	111.6	188.1	331.5
1977	118.9	114.9	210.0	347.8
1978	105.3	117.6	229.7	345.2
1979	129.6	116.4	217.1	427.3
1980	136.6	121.7	192.0	611.3
1981 May	136.2	131.1	201.7	660.7

Source: Calculated from Table 6-4.

increases. Thus the terms of trade changes over these ten years were rather dramatic. It is important also to note that during the 1960s the terms of trade for the same primary products actually fell, though the gains in the 1970s were of staggering proportions and could not have been anticipated by Canadian policy makers. These relatives shifts are summarized in Table 6-5.

On a global scale the terms of trade between resource prices and manufactured goods once again began to shift in favour of industrial production in 1981 and 1982. The evident cause was the world-wide glut of crude oil and the world slump. The federal government's 1981 oil price agreement with Alberta guarantees significantly higher domestic oil prices until 1986, limiting the internal reverse swing of the terms of trade. Since early 1982, when the international oil glut depressed spot prices for crude oil down to around $27-$28 per barrel, the thinking shifted in terms of the timing issue. Canadian domestic prices for "old" oil could reach their maximum with regard to world prices early in 1983.

This chapter is also concerned with the financial intermediation between the various regions and how they may have been affected by these important economic developments, but these flows of funds simply cannot be traced directly. Crude interprovincial trade data are available and are presented here to indicate one facet of the financial recycling process which potentially faced Quebec and Ontario as a result of the relative deterioration of their economic base. The net export statistics found in Table 6-6 indicate that the terms of trade shifts after 1971 contributed to the economic problems of Quebec and Ontario.

For example, since 1973 Quebec's net trade position (which includes foreign trade as well as trade with other provinces) has worsened, while Alberta, British Columbia and Saskatchewan's relative trade position has improved.

These statistics can only be used for crude approximations, but they do indicate the sharp trade gains in the West and some trade deterioration in Quebec. Ironically, Ontario's trade position appears relatively strong in the second half of the 1970s, though no doubt statistics for 1980 and 1981 would show a change in this pattern.

As Norrie and Percy suggest in a discussion paper,[5] these trade data imply that the expected adjustment to the first 1973-74 oil price hike was well underway in the second half of the 1970s and that probably the national banking system in Canada helped to cushion that adjustment. Unfortunately, there are no data available that would show the impact of the second OPEC price shock on the net trade positions, but no doubt the second price rise would translate into a far worse deterioration in the trade position of Quebec and Ontario vis-à-vis the three westernmost provinces.

It should be remembered that under more typical circumstances a deficit-trading region would lose bank reserves to a region where trade surpluses are expanding. In Canada's case, the regions tending towards weaker trade, Quebec and Ontario, have not had to face a multiple contraction of the credit available to consumers and business, which might have been the case had they not had the support of the national banking system in this country. That is, the national banks in Canada have probably helped channel credit back into the Quebec and Ontario

86

TABLE 6-6
NET EXPORTS AND RESIDUAL ERROR OF ESTIMATE IN QUEBEC, ONTARIO AND WESTERN CANADA, SELECTED YEARS
($ millions/% of GPE¹)

Year	PQ		Ont		Man		Sask		Alta		BC		Can	
	$	%	$	%	$	%	$	%	$	%	$	%	$	%
1965	265.5	1.8	1,099.5	4.8	−69.0	−2.8	−153.7	−6.0	−99.4	−2.3	−387.2	−6.7	−463.9	−0.8
1970	1,743.4	7.9	1,928.2	5.0	−104.4	−2.9	163.7	5.5	113.1	1.5	−375.0	−4.1	1,878.9	2.1
1973	−278.5	−9.2	2,775.9	5.3	−109.2	−2.0	679.7	14.3	995.3	8.8	224.4	1.5	1,924.5	1.5
1975	−2,182.3	−5.4	1,859.6	2.8	−182.7	−2.6	668.7	9.4	3,025.8	16.1	−182.5	−0.9	−1,079.5	−0.6
1976	−715.7	−1.5	3,955.4	5.2	−382.9	−4.8	−100.5	−1.3	1,373.1	6.4	−248.8	−1.1	−442.2	−0.2
1977	−1,508.3	−3.0	3,947.0	4.7	−815.9	−9.7	136.9	1.6	1,972.4	8.1	310.0	1.2	−361.8	−0.2
1978	−445.5	−0.8	4,581.1	5.1	−437.6	−4.7	397.8	4.2	1,634.6	5.8	331.2	1.2	1,237.7	0.5
1979	−1,106.6	−1.7	6,397.6	6.3	−296.3	−2.9	791.4	7.1	2,216.2	6.5	784.8	2.4	3,094.6	1.1
Simple Average (%) 1975-79	−2.5		4.8		−4.9		4.7		8.6		0.6		0.6	

Note: ¹ GPE = Gross provincial expenditure.

Source: Statistics Canada, *Provincial Economic Accounts Experiment Data 1963-78* (Cat. No. 13-213), February 1981.

economies, and have permitted the support of the newly-emerging deficit-trading situations in other parts of the country as well.

Federal fiscal financial policies, through their transfer programs and other schemes, have also served to cushion the income losses to the slower growth regions as a result of the terms of trade movement. But by and large the natural resource revenue windfalls remain outside of the federal-provincial fiscal equalization system, and this represents from the perspective of eastern Canada a serious economic loss.

Capital market developments and government tax and expenditure policies, however, must not be viewed in isolation from each other. Thus the relative shift in provincial economic prospects resulted in sharp changes in the provincial revenue earnings and expenditures flows. In the 1970s Alberta, the principal winner in the terms of trade situation, earned vast gains in royalties and corporate and personal taxes related to its growing petroleum wealth, and all this increased that province's fiscal strengths while the eastern provinces and the federal government experienced parallel fiscal losses. The leverage these revenues provided — Alberta in particular was able to improve the economic situation of its residents through generous public expenditure policies or tax rate reductions — is one of the concerns facing the less advantaged regions.

For example, back in 1972 the Alberta government spent $894 per capita in the province, only slightly in excess of the Ontario government figure of $813 per capita. Six years later the per capita expenditures in the two provinces were $3,362 in Alberta and $1,654 in Ontario, Alberta's per capita expenditures being roughly double those of Ontario. Alberta does not impose a provincial sales tax and Alberta's income tax per capita was considerably lower than Ontario's, even though personal incomes in Alberta exceed those in Ontario. All in all, the Alberta fiscal position is very strong today and its tax rates and expenditures policies place that province in a very advantageous position for attracting individuals and investment. These data are presented in Table 6-7.

The Alberta Heritage Fund and the Provincial Competition for Industry

The Alberta Heritage Savings and Trust Fund has been the focus of much attention because of its rapid growth and political visibility. In its founding legislation, the Alberta government set aside 30 per cent of its non-renewable resource revenues (principally oil and gas royalties and land sale bonus payments) to be "invested for the benefit of the

TABLE 6-7
SELECTED SOURCES OF PROVINCIAL REVENUE AND GROSS EXPENDITURES PER CAPITA
(Estimated)

	Nfld	PEI	NS	NB	PQ	Ont	Man	Sask	Alta	BC	All Prov.
1978-79											
Personal income tax per capita	269	212	298	284	705	406	373	349	307	436	465
General sales tax per capita	282	190	160	190	204	207	144	163	—	238	187
Gross government expenditures per capita	2,065	2,200	1,745	1,873	2,227	1,654	1,692	2,112	3,362	1,901	2,020
1976-77											
Personal income tax per capita	193	146	208	216	579	266	285	301	239	294	348
General sales tax per capita	251	167	166	167	215	216	178	187	—	273	199
Gross government expenditures per capita	1,674	1,794	1,458	1,522	1,787	1,417	1,022	1,766	1,838	1,662	1,665
1972-73											
Personal income tax per capita	62	56	100	86	211	151	143	83	135	135	153
General sales tax per capita	106	106	103	101	117	109	87	81	—	100	99
Gross government expenditures per capita	1,037	970	773	887	863	813	731	702	894	710	838

Source: Canadian Tax Foundation, *Provincial and Municipal Finances* (Toronto, 1979), in Norrie and Percy, "Westward Shift and Interregional Adjustment," p. 129A.

people of Alberta in future years.'' The fund's objectives were to strengthen and diversify the economy and to improve the quality of life. In the longer term, it was thought that the fund could provide income and possibly even capital to make up for the government revenue losses that would occur once oil began to run out.

The Heritage Fund currently as six divisions: Capital Projects, Canadian Investment, Alberta Investment, Energy Investment, Commercial Investment and Marketable Securities. Thus far the investment direction of the Heritage Fund has been rather conservative. In 1981 the fund's $8.6 billion in assets were distributed in the following way: 53 per cent to the Alberta Investment Division, 11 per cent to the Capital Projects Division, and 17 per cent to the Canadian Investment Division. The Marketable Securities Division, which owned $1.3 billion of government fixed-income securities and short-term instruments, held 15 per cent of assets. The funds in the Alberta Investment Division were to be used by the government to broaden the province's economic base. Consequently the fund undertakes direct debt or equity participation in major energy projects, such as the Alaska Highway Pipeline. A new Energy Investment Division and a Commercial Investment Division were established in 1980, though expenditures as at year-end 1980 were modest. No Commercial Investment expenditures showed up in the 1981 Annual Report.

The fund's managers have been widely criticized for investing their funds heavily in provincial and government bonds where losses have been earned because of high interest rates.

Several aspects about the Alberta Heritage Fund are important to note. First of all, it is not only large, but is also expected to grow at a fairly quick pace as Canadian energy prices move towards world levels. Indeed, Tom Sindlinger, a member of the Alberta legislative assembly, estimates that the Heritage Fund could grow to $22.3 billion by 1985 and $50.3 billion by 1990, assuming the present allocation of 30 per cent of Alberta's natural resource revenues continues to flow into the fund. But an increase in that allocation percentage could easily see the fund rise to $50 billion by 1983.[6] Tables 6-8 and 6-9 highlight the distribution of the fund's assets in 1980 and 1981, and the objectives of the various divisions.

There is no justification to believe that the Canadian capital markets (on a regional basis) will behave any less efficiently because of the growth of economic and political power in western Canada, and in particular because of the large pool of funds in the Alberta Heritage Fund.

90

TABLE 6-8
ALBERTA HERITAGE SAVINGS TRUST FUND BALANCE SHEET,
MARCH 31, 1980, 1981
($000s)

	1980 ($)	1981 ($)	Distribution in 1981 %
Assets:			
Deposit in the Consolidated Cash Investment			
Trust Fund of the Province of Alberta	44,116	42,857	0.5
Accrued interest and accounts receivable	145,598	222,248	2.6
Due from the General Revenue Fund			
of the Province of Alberta	—	22,670	0.3
Marketable securities	1,427,007	1,290,746	15.0
Canada Investment Division investments	928,513	1,491,923	17.4
Alberta Investment Division investments	3,140,311	4,523,857	52.7
Energy Investment Division investments	—	25,000	0.3
	5,685,545	7,619,301	88.8
Deemed Assets:			
Capital Projects Division investments	733,435	960,508	11.2
	6,418,980	8,579,809	

Source: Alberta Heritage Savings Trust Fund, 1980-81 Annual Report.

TABLE 6-9
THE ALBERTA HERITAGE SAVINGS TRUST FUND—ORGANIZATION

Division	Objectives	Investment Criteria	Maximum Share of Fund's Assets (Actual Share March 31, 1981)
Marketable securities	Investment in high quality securities (money market instruments, corp. and prov. bonds)	Highest yield consistent with risk	Residual (15%)
Canada investment	Loans to fed. and prov. govts and entities where debt is govt guaranteed	Loans at market interest rates	20% (17.4%)
Alberta investment	Strengthen and diversify Alberta economy	Must achieve objectives and yield reasonable return to fund	No limit (52.7%)
Energy	Facilitate the development, processing or transportation of energy resources within Canada	Yield reasonable return or profit to fund	No limit (0.3%)
Commercial investment	A broad class of eligible investments (including equities)	Yield a commercial return or profit to fund	No announced limit (thus far no expenditures)
Capital projects	Long-term benefits to Albertans	Projects which will not yield a return of capital or income to fund	20% (1.2%)

From the efficiency perspective most experts are quite sanguine with respect to the fund. Andrew G. Kniewasser, President of the Investment Dealers Association of Canada, suggested that "The fund is not a drag on the economy of Alberta nor the economy of Canada. It is a large pool of real savings which is fueling the Canadian capital market every day. It is a pool of savings and investment, much of it is in a liquid form, which can be committed to longer-term investment opportunities as they arise in Alberta and in Canada. The fund is fully invested and is working for Alberta and for Canada every day."[7] The same writer was very optimistic about the Canadian capital market as well. "We are fortunate to have in Canada the best capital market of any country in the world. Our mechanism for matching up savings and investment outperform those of any other country. For example, we raise on a relative basis through securities market, twice as much new financing in Canada as in the United States."[8]

But Thomas J. Courchene and James R. Melvin have observed that the fund carries with it a new political dimension. The fund is not only growing rapidly but is also "in a privileged position vis-à-vis private sector enterprises and as such it places these latter institutions at a distinct disadvantage."[9] That is, Alberta's new-found affluence could allow that province to out-compete all other provinces for future investment property. It is clear that if it chose to, Alberta could (and to some degree it already has) lower tax rates, provide subsidies to municipalities and businesses, and increase the role of the public sector in terms of ownership of private resources.

Indeed, it is in this gray area of economic competition that a real and genuine concern exists. That is, the public sectors of Alberta, Saskatchewan and British Colulmbia could effectively change the cost of capital for business operating in their regions compared with other jurisdictions. In other words there could be micro- rather than macro-oriented economic policy concerns developing, and to judge these issues based on the narrow criteria of efficient responses of interest rates across regions to generally identical conditions would be to miss the main policy issue of the 1980s, the regional competition for investment funds.

Let us provide an illustration of the cost of capital effect. It is well known that in Canada Ontario Hydro with government guarantees can raise funds at a lower rate than Imperial Oil of Canada. This, of course, lowers the cost of capital to Ontario Hydro with respect to Imperial Oil and in turn means that hydroelectric power, which remains within the public sector, has a lower cost of development than private oil development. To some degree this is the real capital markets issue. As well, the Canadian provinces have always been in competition for industry, and now Alberta could use its extra oil-related revenues to make itself more attractive for investment purposes. Thus far, the amount of new competition spurred on by the shift of monies to western Canada has been surprisingly small.

Conclusion

There is a mistaken, widely-held view that in the context of regional economic growth Canada faces a zero-sum game, that one region's gain is another region's loss. The weak economic performance of the two large central provinces of Quebec and Ontario over the past decade can only be indirectly related to western economic gains. As Norrie and Percy correctly argue, the real sources of change are higher oil prices and the price-inelastic demand. The exercise of market power by the OPEC countries which caused the relative price shift has little to do with western Canada. Indeed, the opposite is the case, since the real income problems in eastern Canada would have been far worse if it had not had access to western oil at below world prices.

Norrie and Percy concluded that the western provinces have not been achieving advantages at the expense of the eastern provinces, and that the industrial changes that have taken place thus far simply reflect the faster growth rates of the western provinces rather than structural change.

> There is no firm indication either from the available data that the four western economies are in the midst of diversifying beyond areas of traditional comparative advantage into ones more directly competitive with those of central Canada. The growth in manufacturing and services that is evident seemed to be directly tied to the expansion of the primary sector, especially the energy industries. . . .
> By comparison, the shift [of activity to the west] associated with the opening up of western agricultural lands after 1900 dwarfs the present one.[10]

In the final analysis it is the regional competition for new investment, and the possibility that provincial investment subsidies will create tensions in the 1980s, that will affect the flow of investment. As noted previously, the seeds of this type of regional competition for investment lie as much in the East as in the West. In particular, consider the subsidies that the Ontario and federal governments provided to Ford Motor Company and Massey-Ferguson in 1981. These subsidies were not made for the same reason, but they show that all large firms are aware of how to play one government off against another. All provincial governments are now becoming more heavily involved in the business of providing investment incentives to attract industries.

These shifting economic fortunes are viewed with alarm in some eastern circles and by the federal government. Yet Norrie and Percy in their review of western economic developments concluded that there had been little real economic diversification within the western provinces until 1971; and even since then most of the faster growth in the western provinces has complemented economic growth in eastern Canada. Indeed, they demonstrated that the more rapid economic growth of the western provinces has not, so far, resulted in any fundamental change in the economies of the West. Further, according to Norrie and Percy, the notion that eastern Canada is worse off as a consequence of the latest wave of western prosperity is wrong.

The kind of faster economic growth that has occurred in western Canada would naturally also result in some shift of financial activity to the western provinces. Once again the data are very sketchy on the subject, but it appears that thus far the shifts that have taken place have not been significant. Norrie and Percy provide statistics that show that the regional distribution of directors in the five largest chartered banks did not change much between 1968 and 1978.[11] As to the 100 largest corporations, there has been some increase in western representation among the directorships, but once again this reflects the fact that some rapidly growing western-based companies have recently achieved sufficient size to classify among Canada's top 100 corporations.

At some point, unwarranted provincial government competition for new industry becomes counterproductive and results only in revenue losses to the public purse. For example, David Perry et al. noted in an article in the *Canadian Tax Journal* that a new type of investment subsidy was introduced in the 1979 budgets of the governments of Quebec, Ontario and British Columbia.

> In those provinces, for the first time since the outbreak of World War II, tax measures were proposed which would have the effect of directing savings and capital flows to investments within each province. The measures were explained as incentives for the development of provincial business and no stress was put on the negative aspects, that is, directing funds from other provinces or other countries. To the extent that other provinces or the federal government match these tax measures, the effect should be more to limit foreign investment further. However, as the measures now stand, the possibility of interprovincial

tax competition has been raised. The machinery of federal-provincial consultation exists which could prevent such competition.[12]

Alberta could be gearing up for the more vigorous use of the corporate tax tool as a means of attracting additional firms into the province. Beginning in 1981, Alberta began collecting its own corporation taxes, a device introduced by Ontario back in 1957. Quebec has always collected its own corporation taxes.

As to the issue of subsidies to business, Maxwell and Pestieau[13] compiled a list of provincial protection policies in effect throughout the country in 1980. They felt, based on their analysis, that it would be difficult to argue that there is greater preferential treatment given business in western Canada than in other parts of the country.

In addition, it is difficult to argue that the Heritage Fund has altered capital flows very significantly. Norrie and Percy note that:

> While the assets of the Alberta fund do seem large, especially when the present value of the future receipts is calculated, two points need to be raised here. First, to date at least, the Fund has not been used to directly promote economic diversification. The Pacific Western Airlines purchase and the equity position in the Alberta Energy company are the exceptions rather than the rule. Most of the assets are lent out to other governments, or invested in infrastructure within Alberta, or held as interest bearing assets.[14]

Finally, the Major Projects Task Force has estimated that over the next two decades Canada will spend about $430 billion on investment projects currently on the drawing board, with about 48 per cent of the total investment spending centred in the western provinces including the Yukon and NWT. (See Table 4-2.) Unfortunately too little attention has been given to the heavy investment calendar in eastern Canada. While the megaprojects in western Canada are large-scale and attention-grabbing, they still amount to less spending than is likely to occur in eastern Canada. And even though the West and Alberta reap a disproportionate share of this future wave of investment spending, there are still some positive spin-offs to Ontario because of its geographic location and its pre-eminence in the steel industry, the machine-producing industry and the skilled labour market.

96

Housing Finance: The 1970s and Prospects for the 1980s

7

Introduction

Canada's housing industry has always received a high level of official attention and promotion from federal and provincial governments. Housing is an important economic sector. Aside from the social value of housing, and the large numbers of workers employed in residential construction, it is also fairly labour-intensive and normally utilizes a high proportion of domestic materials in construction. In other words, the multiplier effect of spending on housing is greater for the domestic economy than similar types of expenditures on machinery, automobiles or other consumer goods, which in the past presented seemingly good reasons for favouring this sector of the economy. New residential construction accounts for about 6 per cent of Canada's GNP, but its influence is also very important in the related household durable goods industries and, of course, the financial markets.

But on the other side of the coin an argument has been developed that the housing sector should not receive as much attention in future years as it has in the past, since population projections indicate a sharp decline in the number of new households in the 1980s, and therefore fewer new houses will be required. By international standards Canada is a very well-housed nation, and Canada's future housing requirements, which are related to the formation of new households, is expected to moderate very sharply.

But there is also another consideration which was raised in chapter 1. The Royal Trust flow-of-funds projections indicated that a smooth financing of the megaproject wave of investment in the 1980s would be made easier by the assumed relative shrinkage of the housing industry.

According to estimates based on demographic projections, total new housing requirements amounted to about 237,000 units in 1981 and were expected to decline to about 214,000 units by 1985 and 156,000 units by 1990.[1] That is, the underlying demand for new housing activity in the 1980s is expected to weaken sharply because of demographic trends.

Despite the above demographic trends, housing still remains the centrepiece of economic policy at the provincial level, even if federal government interests are waning. Inflation and associated high mortgage lending rates have been very destructive to the Canadian housing industry, and this explains in part why a housing inflation bubble arose briefly in 1981 in many metropolitan centres across Canada. Further, new housing starts in Canada in 1980 fell to their lowest level since 1966, and the current housing slump is the longest since the 1930s. These developments are usually indicative of a very loose market and of excess supply for housing, a fact made worse by the slump in residential construction which set in after 1976 and which continued on into 1982.

It is widely recognized that high and variable mortgage interest rates discourage access to home ownership, and this chapter will indicate how such an effect operates in practice. At the same time, it must be appreciated that high mortgage rates also affect lending institutions, making them more cautious and resulting in a shortening of the term of the outstanding debt structure.[2] But despite these drawbacks, the typical residential dwelling has represented for most Canadians the only practical inflation hedge available. However, since interest rates became so high in real terms, the inflation hedge effect has become somewhat shaky.

The general decline in housing construction since the mid-1970s has been attributed to both cyclical and secular forces at work. In the multiple-unit field, rent controls became more prevalent during the 1970s as general inflation heated up. The existence of rent controls, imposed at the provincial level after 1975 in conjunction with the Anti-Inflation Board program, created a series of housing market distortions in the multiple unit dwelling market. Thus it is no surprise that investors avoid committing their funds in this area, and that when shortages of rental dwelling units developed, governments were forced to respond with other measures designed to rechannel investment funds into the apartment dwelling market.

E. Wayne Clendenning, in a study published in November 1980,[3] indicated that imbalances between rental construction and owner-occupied construction can be traced to the introduction of the federal Assisted Home Ownership Plan (AHOP) in 1973. That plan, which provided interest payment grants, was followed by an Assisted Rental Program in April 1975, which provided grants or interest-free loans to encourage rental construction. Further, the Canadian rental market came under a series of provincially-imposed rent controls in late 1975 and in 1976 which varied in intensity and coverage among the provinces. Rental construction in 1982 is still limited, and rent controls exist in all provinces except Alberta and Manitoba, although they are slated to be reintroduced in Manitoba in 1982.

Rental construction was so badly hurt as a result of these controls that the Multiple Unit Rental Building (MURB) tax incentives were continued for much of the last half-decade. These incentives provided substantial capital cost allowance advantage to developers to encourage multiple unit residential building construction. Under these initiatives, tax payers who invested in rental properties were allowed to deduct their capital cost allowance and certain "soft" costs against income from other sources. The MURB tax incentives were removed in the November 1981 federal budget.

As a general proposition, it is probably accurate to assert that the negative effect of rent controls on the construction of new multiple unit residential dwellings becomes even more exaggerated as the rate of inflation heats up. Indeed, in a rather perverse way, high inflation guarantees the continuance of provincially-imposed rent controls which in themselves have been a major impediment to the rental construction market.

Demographic developments can be considered another longer-term force which slowed the underlying demand for new residential construction in the second half of the 1970s. Supporting this proposition is a Canada Mortgage and Housing Corporation (CMHC) demographic projection of new family and non-family households at various periods of time. The rate of increase of household formation had been slowing during the 1970s, and a natural peaking-out is predicted on the CMHC statistics for the early 1980s. A decided downturn in the household formation level is expected from that point on right through to the middle 1990s.

Thus inflation and financial bottlenecks contributed to a social cleavage between families who already owned homes and who earned substantial capital gains, those who had recently purchased homes and were struggling to remain financially solvent in 1981 and 1982, and those who were not yet homeowners or could not afford to become one.

It is clear that the slowing of household formation levels during the second half of the 1970s probably eased some of the pressures on overall residential construction growth — though if these statistics portend the near future, the underlying housing demand should decline much further in terms of new units to be constructed.

Finally, high inflation and high interest rates in particular have altered the economics of housing finance. Despite the fact that housing has been an appropriate inflation hedge over the past quarter-century, not everyone has had the ability to take advantage of it.

Even in the high mortgage rate environment of the late 1970s and the early 1980s, the carrying costs or the occupancy costs of housing investments tended to decline in real terms because of the rapid rate of housing inflation. In part this was due to the fact that inflation in housing has tended to exceed the general rate of inflation over time, although housing prices seem to move more in discontinuous leaps compared with the smoother general inflation indexes. Another way of stating this is to review real mortgage interest rate trends, which over much of the 1970s resulted in significant lender subsidies to borrowers.

Housing Finance in the 1970s

It is interesting to review the figures presented in Tables 7-1 and 7-2 to consider how the composition of housing finance in Canada has changed over the last decade. In 1970, for example, lending institutions in Canada approved $2.7 billion in new mortgage loans, and $1.4 billion of that total, or 51.8 per cent, was allocated to the finance of new residential dwellings. (See Table 7-1.) By 1979 new mortgage approvals amounted to $17.2 billion, while the financing of new housing construction rose to $5.6 billion, although proportionately this represented only 32.6 per cent of total new mortgage financing activities. These two years, 1970 and 1979, were not strong years for Canada's housing market; new units under construction amounted to 190,500 in 1970 and 197,000 in 1979. In contrast, a peak level of activity was reached in 1976, with 268,500 new residential units under construction; yet the mortgage financing allocated to new construction in that year amounted to only 53.2 per cent out of the total residential financing.

In a nutshell, these data indicate that the relative importance of new housing finance within the mortgage market declined during the 1970s, even though new residential expenditures as a percentage of GNP increased from 4.1 per cent in 1970 to 5.3 per cent in 1979. This dichotomy in part reveals a reaction to the fact that housing inflation increased so swiftly on existing units. If new unit construction in coming years moderates more or less in line with the demographic projections cited earlier, then the new residential market financing will shrink relatively much more in the 1980s than it did in the 1970s.

The other important part of the residential construction market that

100

deserves attention is the financing for multiple unit dwellings. In 1959 multiple unit dwellings, defined to include semi-detached houses, duplexes, row houses and apartments, made up 34.8 per cent of total

TABLE 7-1

MORTGAGE LOANS APPROVED BY LENDING INSTITUTIONS [1]
BY TYPE OF LENDER, CANADA, SELECTED YEARS, 1970-80
($000's)

Year	Chartered Banks	Life Insurance Cos	Trust Cos	Loan[2] Cos	Other[3] Cos	Total
		NEW RESIDENTIAL CONSTRUCTION				
1970	379,114	177,202	544,524	200,072	95,822	1,396,734
1975	1,570,769	562,068	1,484,711	902,818	156,369	4,676,735
1979	1,937,890	822,882	1,370,346	1,207,403	232,466	5,568,987
1980	1,619,015	704,231	1,113,286	721,018	225,727	4,383,277
		EXISTING RESIDENTIAL PROPERTY				
1970	114,130	38,655	347,028	185,446	37,824	723,083
1975	1,216,100	190,032	1,807,807	1,022,544	92,725	4,329,208
1979	3,269,191	416,197	2,957,330	1,689,126	148,086	8,474,930
1980	2,800,137	559,026	2,636,133	1,298,476	149,393	7,443,165
		NON-RESIDENTIAL PROPERTY				
1970	16,538	239,993	188,787	62,299	256	507,873
1975	66,437	758,058	211,460	252,316	1,244	1,289,515
1979	304,834	1,626,318	703,993	506,570	763	3,142,478
1980	324,051	1,219,969	448,804	363,730	993	2,351,547
		TOTAL				
1970	509,782	455,850	1,080,339	447,817	133,902	2,627,690
1975	2,853,306	1,510,158	3,503,978	2,177,678	250,338	10,295,458
1979	5,542,272	2,874,425	5,041,311	3,425,073	392,499	17,275,580
1980	4,765,043	2,491,796	4,210,022	2,406,964	388,961	14,262,786

Notes: [1] Data are gross.
[2] Includes some companies which are wholly-owned subsidiaries of individual banks.
[3] Includes Quebec savings banks, mutual benefit and fraternal societies, pension funds and mortgage investment brokers.

Source: Canada Mortgage and Housing Corporation, *Canadian Housing Statistics 1980*, (Ottawa: CMHC, March 1981), Table 33.

TABLE 7-2
NHA AND CONVENTIONAL MORTGAGE LOANS APPROVED BY LENDING INSTITUTIONS,[2] BY TYPE OF LENDER, CANADA, SELECTED YEARS, 1964-80
(Dwelling Units)

Year	Chartered Banks	Life Insurance Cos	Trust Cos	Loan[2] Cos	Other[3] Cos	Total
		NEW RESIDENTIAL CONSTRUCTION				
1964	886	65,367	25,308	24,160	6,401	122,122
1967	8,435	42,909	25,926	13,707	4,763	95,740
1970	21,938	13,103	36,465	15,110	8,202	94,818
1975	47,545	21,632	46,182	28,396	7,350	151,105
1979	38,563	20,516	32,786	25,180	6,924	123,969
1980	26,709	13,773	22,439	13,603	6,386	82,910
		EXISTING RESIDENTIAL PROPERTY				
1964	—	21,934	29,926	31,000	10,975	93,835
1967	7,317	12,602	23,951	18,596	3,574	66,040
1970	7,013	3,902	27,313	17,796	7,449	63,473
1975	47,352	11,631	73,446	45,266	7,699	185,394
1979	83,018	18,748	102,270	53,049	7,437	262,522
1980	66,122	22,673	82,960	38,918	7,518	218,191
		TOTAL				
1964	886	87,301	55,234	55,160	17,376	215,957
1967	15,752	55,511	49,877	32,303	8,337	161,780
1970	28,951	17,005	63,778	32,906	15,651	158,291
1975	94,897	33,263	119,628	73,662	15,049	336,499
1979	121,581	39,264	133,056	78,229	14,361	386,491
1980	92,831	36,446	105,339	53,521	13,904	301,101

Notes: [1] Data are gross.
[2] Includes some companies which are wholly-owned subsidiaries of individual banks.
[3] Includes Quebec savings banks, mutual benefit and fraternal societies, pension funds and mortgage investment brokers.

Source: Canada Mortgage and Housing Corporation, *Canadian Housing Statistics 1980* (Ottawa: CMHC, March 1981), Table 34.

dwelling units started. That proportion rose to 62.7 per cent by 1969 but had declined to 44.6 per cent by 1979. Not all multiple unit dwellings are rental properties per se. CMHC statistics indicate that in

1959 37,000 apartment units were constructed in Canada; this total rose to 111,000 by 1969 and fell to 58,000 units by 1979. Apartment construction activity peaked out in 1973, and by 1979 had declined by 45 per cent from the 1973 levels. In contrast, non-apartment unit construction remained more stable, with levels of 162,000 in 1973 and 138,000 in 1979.[4]

It is apparent, then, that there is a mixture of longer-run secular, cyclical and institutional forces affecting the mortgage financing trends. In the early 1970s, real mortgage interest rates, measured as the difference between nominal (or actual) mortgage interest rates less the prevailing rate of inflation, were historically low. As well, the supply of funds available to the mortgage market seemed ample, particularly as the chartered banks began to move into this financing area after the 1967 Bank Act revision. Further, the Canadian labour force was growing rapidly in the 1970s, aided by rising female labour force participation rates. This in effect brought many more double-income families into the housing market. Housing inflation was somewhat erratic in the 1970s, and because of high real interest rates and the price escalation on new and existing houses, we find ourselves in 1982 with potentially an excess demand for housing.

The Impact of Selected Government Programs on Residential Construction

Earlier it was argued that rent controls represent a serious distortion to the housing market, a distortion that has spurred on provincial and federal initiatives to compensate for the controls, laying distortion upon distortion. Yet political considerations make the removal of provincially-based rent controls even less likely with very high inflation. The factor that has drastically changed in recent years is inflation, and its direct effect in causing higher mortgage interest rates. The housing industry is truly facing a crisis in Canada, one that, when examined realistically, has less to do with the functioning of the financial markets than with the reality that inflation causes higher mortgage interest rates; and since the Bank of Canada emphasizes high interest rates as a means of dampening inflation, the combination of inflation and monetary policy tends to make the housing industry much more cyclically prone. That is, in this writer's view, the problem facing the housing industry is caused not by a failure of the financial markets or the mortgage markets, but rather by the failure of the federal government effectively to reduce Canada's high inflation rate.

The slump in new residential construction is made worse by inflation interacting with existing rent controls, which limit the construction of rental dwelling units. Even with additional "supplemental" tax incentives and/or housing subsidies, the incentive to invest in rental accommodation was, and is, simply not adequate. For example, the CMHC estimated that in 1981 the net increment in rental unit construction which could be traced directly to its MURB program amounted to only about 10,000 units.[5] The Registered Home Ownership Savings Plan (the RHOSP program) provides a considerable incentive to the household sector to accumulate and direct non-taxable savings, at a faster pace than it might otherwise, to the housing investment field, though it is difficult to estimate the impact of this fiscal subsidy on housing demand.

In 1979 the federal government subsidy to MURB construction amounted to $45 million as estimated in terms of the tax expenditures resulting from the implicit reduction of its personal income tax revenues. That is, in 1979 Ottawa invested $45 million of deferred taxes in the housing industry because the government felt that multiple unit construction was too low. Yet the reason why multiple unit construction was retarded in Canada was that the advantage to the investor was simply not there. The tax expenditure costs to the federal government of the RHOSP program have averaged nearly $100 million annually in the personal income tax system since the mid-1970s.[6]

The Latest Housing Slump

There is no doubt that there is much to the argument that unusually high "real" interest rates have hurt first-house purchasers, and have resulted in the latest slump in residential construction. The CMHC noted in a *Quarterly Housing Outlook and Economic Forecast* published in February 1981 that the then "four-year decline in new residential activity represents the longest continuing downturn since the 1929-33 period. Compared to the level of 197,049 units for 1979, 1980 starts were 19.5 per cent lower and, in comparison with the record high of 273,203 units in 1976, the decline amounted to 42 per cent."[7]

With these declines in the residential sector, it is estimated that the construction industry was utilizing only 60 to 70 per cent of its capacity throughout 1980.

The CMHC noted in the same report that the long-term decline in the new residential construction industry, which was supposed to have been based on demographics, may have actually begun half a decade earlier than forecast because of the interaction between demographic forces and the very high interest rates.

The 1982 housing outlook is even more grim. There seems virtually no incentives for private developers to build any new rental units. Despite a virtually zero vacancy rate in the apartment market in Toronto and elsewhere, few new buildings are being planned in 1982. The problem here relates to an adverse combination of high mortgage financing costs, rent controls, and the exceptional wariness of the development industry of investing in Canada because of the disincentives introduced in the 1981 federal budget.

The Impact of Higher Mortgage Interest Rates on First-Home Purchasers

In 1980, the CMHC published a brief study which identified some of the negative effects of higher mortgage costs on a family's ability to purchase its first home.[8] The report also provided a rough calculation of the number of households in major metropolitan cities that were priced out of the housing market because of rising mortgage costs in 1979. The uneven incidence on first-home buyers from rising mortgage rates is due to a combination of two factors: housing price differentials and income level differences across Canada. For example, in 1979 an average-priced house sold for $46,131 in Montreal, $70,831 in Toronto and $82,428 in Calgary. Yet income variations between the major cities in 1979 were not as pronounced as the variations in housing prices. This fact alone helps explain why higher mortgage interest rates had a much harsher impact on first-house purchasers living in the high-priced market areas such as Calgary, Edmonton and Vancouver. Tables 7-3 and 7-4 present the data that support these arguments.

If one begins with the assumption that first-time house buyers typically have little cash for a down payment, then their capacity to purchase a house is primarily determined by the amount of mortgage debt they can carry relative to the size of the family income. Consequently, a rise in either housing prices or mortgage interest rates reduces the access to home ownership by reducing the number of households that can qualify for mortgage financing.

By assuming a 30 per cent gross debt service (GDS) ratio and an 11 per cent mortgage rate, the CMHC study noted that in 1979 an income of $32,300 was required to purchase an average-priced house of $82,000 in Calgary. In contrast, the lower average-priced house in Montreal ($46,000) required only a $19,200 family income.

TABLE 7-3
COMPARISON[1] OF INCOMES REQUIRED[2] TO AFFORD
AN AVERAGE-PRICED HOUSE[3] AT VARIOUS MORTGAGE
INTEREST RATES, BY SELECTED METROPOLITAN AREAS, 1979
($)

Metropolitan Area	Average House Price	Income Required at Various Interest Rates			
		9%	11%	13%	15%
St. John's	44,561	16,200	18,500	20,900	23,300
Halifax	47,154	17,200	19,600	22,100	24,700
Saint John	42,324	15,400	17,600	19,800	22,200
Montreal	46,131	16,800	19,200	21,600	24,100
Hamilton	53,787	19,600	22,400	25,200	28,200
Kitchener	54,925	20,000	22,900	25,800	28,800
Sudbury	45,308	16,500	18,800	21,200	23,700
Toronto	70,831	25,100	28,600	32,200	36,000
Windsor	53,339	19,500	22,200	25,000	27,900
Winnipeg	48,408	17,700	20,100	22,700	25,300
Regina	47,268	17,200	19,700	22,200	24,700
Saskatoon	56,019	20,400	23,300	26,300	29,300
Calgary	82,428	28,400	32,300	36,400	40,600
Edmonton	78,852	27,500	31,300	35,300	39,400
Vancouver	78,902	27,500	31,400	35,300	39,400

Notes: [1] Estimates based on 1974 Survey of Housing Units. Household incomes and the number of households were inflated to 1979.

[2] The calculations are based on the following parameters and/or assumptions:
  (a) Mortgage amounts are set equal to the loan amount allowed under the NHA.
  (b) Income requirements are based on gross debt service (GDS) ratio of 30 per cent and a level payment mortgage instrument.
  (c) Property taxes are assumed to represent 1.5 per cent of house price.

[3] Based on average MLS house prices in 1979.

Source: Canadian Mortgage and Housing Corporation, *Special Report: Effect of Interest Rate Changes on Affordability of Housing By Market User* (Ottawa: CMHC, 1980).

As mortgage rates rose in Canada in 1979, the level of family income necessary to purchase a house also rose. But the differences in the minimum family income required in order to purchase a house across regions become more pronounced with higher mortgage interest rates. For example, using 1979 statistics, if mortgage interest rates rose from 11 to 15 per cent, it would require a family income increase of $8,300 to purchase an average-priced house in Calgary compared with family income increase of $5,000 to purchase an average house in Montreal.

On the face of it, this might be somewhat surprising, but the effect

TABLE 7-4
INCIDENCE OF RENTERS[1] WHO CAN AFFORD[2] AN AVERAGE-PRICED HOUSE[3] AT VARIOUS MORTGAGE INTEREST RATES, BY SELECTED METROPOLITAN AREAS, 1979

Metropolitan Area	Total Number[4] of Households in CMA	% of Households That Can Afford Average-Priced House at Various Interest Rates			
		9%	11%	13%	15%
St. John's	9,900	54.7	45.8	38.1	31.9
Halifax	33,600	56.9	46.0	36.2	27.9
Saint John	10,800	54.1	43.3	34.4	26.2
Montreal	369,500	53.5	47.1	37.3	30.7
Hamilton	41,300	44.0	33.1	24.8	15.0
Kitchener	29,300	43.0	33.7	23.9	16.5
Sudbury	14,100	62.0	53.0	39.8	33.1
Toronto	288,400	37.6	26.2	17.0	10.4
Windsor	15,900	48.0	41.3	30.5	21.1
Winnipeg	56,300	39.6	29.7	24.1	16.0
Regina	12,600	39.3	31.2	26.5	19.1
Saskatoon	12,300	30.6	22.6	15.3	9.9
Calgary	53,500	17.3	10.7	6.9	4.4
Edmonton	69,700	19.9	14.0	9.4	6.1
Vancouver	129,600	20.8	13.9	10.0	6.6
Total of 15 areas No. of households	1,146,800	464,500	368,700	276,100	205,600
% of all households	100.0	40.5	32.2	24.1	17.9

Notes: [1] Estimates based on 1974 Survey of Housing Units. Household incomes and the number of households were inflated to 1979. Household heads are less than 45 years of age.
[2] The calculations are based on the following parameters and/or assumptions:
   (a) Mortgage amounts are set equal to the loan amount allowed under the NHA.
   (b) Income requirements are based on gross debt service (GDS) ratio of 30 per cent and a level payment mortgage instrument.
   (c) Property taxes are assumed to represent 1.5 per cent of house price.
[3] Based on average MLS house prices in 1979.
[4] Renter households with head less than 45 years of age.

Source: Canada Mortgage and Housing Corporation, *Special Report: Effect of Interest Rate Change on Affordability of Housing By Market Area* (Ottawa: CMHC, 1980).

of higher mortgage interest rates are potentially harsher in the existing high-priced housing markets than in the low-priced areas. In the fifteen metropolitan areas the CMHC study singled out for attention, some 369,000 families could purchase an average-priced house at an 11 per cent mortgage rate in 1979; a rise in the mortgage rate to 15 per cent cut that number to 206,000 families, a decline of 44 per cent. But the decline in the potential client list is far more severe in the high-priced Calgary market than in the relatively low-priced Montreal market.

In conclusion, it is clear that the effect of higher mortgage interest rates on reducing access to first-home purchases is more severe in the high-priced housing markets than in the low-priced markets. Even under normal conditions, the effects of higher housing prices in Calgary, Edmonton and Vancouver lower the access to house purchases at any fixed mortgage rate for renters living in those market areas. That is, the percentage of households that can afford an average-priced house in the high-priced areas is significantly smaller than in the low-priced areas. Increases in mortgage interest rates such as were seen in 1981 only compound the problem of potential house purchasers living in high-priced housing markets.

Problems with Refinancing and Mortgage Rollovers

The shortening of the maturity of mortgages was an expected response to the higher and more variable inflation rates and interest rates. Mortgage rate negotiations over the past five years have occurred at ever higher interest rates at a time when real family income growth was slowing because of adverse national economic developments. Not surprisingly, the interest rate sensitive housing industry seemed to accept the brunt of tighter monetary conditions, as new flows of residential construction contracted, and Canada's housing industry experienced a slump because of higher real interest rates and the continuance of housing inflation. In some metropolitan centres, housing prices on existing property more than tripled over the 1970s, compared with about a doubling in the cost of living indexes. Yet the MLS listings across the country illustrate on average only about a doubling of housing prices between 1970 and 1980, a rate of increase that does not seem so outlandish relative to general inflation.

The mortgage rollover problem has been a shock to individuals who were forced to renegotiate at higher rates over the last half-decade; indeed rollovers have at times doubled the effective mortgage rates. The conventional mortgage rate escalated sharply since the early 1970s and reached a peak of over 20 per cent at one point in 1981. This was more than double the level of the mortgage interest rates that prevailed in the late 1960s. But while high interest rates and the housing inflation cycle have created a liquidity problem, the value of the housing asset has on the whole kept up with general inflation. Thus despite hardships in some cases because of higher mortgage costs, the wealth position of the hard-pressed homeowner has been maintained. Their problems cannot be judged as serious as the financing problems of those who have never entered the marketplace before and who might be kept perpetually out of the house ownership market.

In the case of a first-house purchaser, the market has responded with a series of potentially ingenious financing devices, although some correctly regard these devices as simply gimmicks. In a real income protection sense, the first-house buyer cannot protect his real asset position unless he has been involved in the housing market.

Two other factors seem to be at work with respect to this issue. First, home ownership is still the preferred form of housing tenure, despite the high cost of mortgage money, and as our experience with high mortgage interest rates continues, buyers' resistance to high mortgage rates might ease. Secondly, some of the housing industry financing problems can be traced to the introduction of well-meaning but ill-conceived programs to increase the access of home ownership to low-income individuals. Is this really a financial market failure or is it rather a failure of general economic policies to provide sufficient income to all groups of Canadians?

Conclusion

In conclusion, Canada's housing industry has always occupied an important place in the public policy arena. Although residential construction contributes only about 6 per cent to Canada's GNP, this sector's share of public policy attention has always loomed far larger than its GNP representation. This chapter notes that, on average, housing inflation has exceeded general inflation in the 1970s (particularly on existing property), but that since 1976 high mortgage interest rates have caused the longest residential construction slump since the 1930s. Rental construction has experienced a series of particular problems, most acutely because of the introduction of provincial rent controls in 1975.

Clearly it would be in the interests of the general public if rent controls could be fully phased out. Within the rental market, the problem has been diagnosed from a tenant's perspective as one of too high a price for accommodation. One could alternatively view the problem as one of income insufficiency. Viewed from this perspective, the income transfer mechanism seems the more proper route for assisting those facing what appear to be exorbitant rental rates.

Introducing a specifically targeted shelter allowance might be one way of beginning the process of dismantling rent controls.

In the 1970s layer upon layer of government programs were introduced to assist the poor to purchase housing and to encourage investors to construct multiple unit dwellings for rental purposes. Yet the financing of housing construction was constrained because of high interest rates, inflation and its rationing effect on house purchasers.

Since the 1967 Bank Act, the chartered banks and the mortgage loan companies — many of which are wholly-owned subsidiaries of the individual banks — have overtaken the trust companies and the life insurance companies in the mortgage lending market. The banks and mortgage loan companies' proportion of total new residential mortgage lending rose between 1970 and 1979 from 41.5 to 56.4 per cent of total financing, while their proportion of financing on existing properties rose from 41.4 to 58.5 per cent. Inflation and the 1967 Bank Act have been kind to the chartered banks in one particular sense. Inflation has essentially dried up the long-term corporate bond market, which has meant that business borrowing has backed disproportionately into the banking system, while at the same time the banks have expanded their market base in the mortgage field.

With inflation continuing at such a high level, it is not surprising that the terms to maturity of mortgage debt have shortened, adding to the uncertainty of mortgage finance. The five-year mortgage had pretty well become the norm in Canada in the 1970s, but when credit became particularly tight on several occasions in 1980 and 1981 it was difficult to negotiate terms of even up to one year's duration. The main point is that it is too disruptive for all concerned when the terms of mortgages continuously shrink as they have over the past several years. Individual families can be whipsawed if their renegotiation occurs when mortgage rates are high and when terms are short.

The private markets and the institutional lenders (both public and private) have adjusted to this new, shortened term structure of debt by developing a variety of new types of mortgage interest instruments designed to entice the first-home purchaser. These new mortgage instruments range all the way from variable interest rate mortgages, to non-amortizing mortgages, to gradualistic payment mortgages and to shared appreciation mortgages. But they all have one feature in common: although they appear to lower interest payments, at least temporarily, in fact over time these interest payments must be made up.

Variable interest rate mortgages provide short-term rollovers of existing contracts with the added protection that the borrower cannot have the contract called if short-term interest rates change very quickly. Open mortgages are mortgages that can be repaid at any time. With non-amortizing mortgages, which were introduced in 1979, the payments are made only for interest, with no payment going to principal. In some gradual payment mortgages, the first-year mortgage payments may amount to only 75 per cent, for example, of the level of an equal-payment mortgage plan, and borrowers have the opportunity to wait for their incomes to rise over time as average mortgage payments rise. Over twenty-five years, according to the CMHC, this type of loan will still cost 10 per cent more than an average loan. Finally, there are the shared appreciation mortgage plans which provide borrowers with a low interest rate in exchange for parting with part of their capital gains from their household unit.

None of these plans overcome the reality that high "real" mortgage interest rates must ultimately be paid, but they do indicate that the combination of ingenious plans and government assistance can still keep housing construction going in an era of unreasonable interest rates. It is clear that interest rate stability and lower interest rates generally would remove the difficulties and uncertainties facing first-house buyers.

Pension Policies and the Canadian Capital Markets

8

Introduction

The main focus of this chapter is on the interaction between private employer-sponsored pension funds, public pension funds and the capital markets in the 1980s. The interface will occur through a series of channels.

Private pension funds are the recipients of savings from the private sector and invest these savings in financial instruments which yield a financial rate of return. Further, the real value of these accumulated savings has been and will continue to be eroded by inflation. Thus the private pension fund system is part of the capital market and interacts with other sectors in the market through its acquisition of particular assets, its competition with other financial intermediaries for savings, and through the pressures of government which has an interest to see that these savings plans are well managed and are able to deliver real purchasing power benefits to retirees.

Publicly-managed social security funds have a similar type of capital market interaction. They are also the recipients of private sector savings and they accumulate these savings either to invest them in securities or to pay off pension benefits directly. Inflation is also a problem for the social security plans, though by legislation the value of CPP/QPP pension benefits are automatically adjusted for rising prices. One other major difference between social security pension funds and employer-sponsored pension funds is that they operate on vastly different funding principles. The Canadian social security plans (CPP/QPP) are only partially funded on an actuarial basis, while private employer-sponsored plans are by necessity and by law fully funded.

Pension policies are now the subject of interest. After several years of intensive study, which concluded with a series of federal and provincial meetings, the entire private and public pension system is up for review. A number of important studies have been published which are expected to influence provincial and federal legislation on pension fund arrangements. One of the latest bodies to report was The Royal Commission on the Status of Pensions in Ontario.[1]

Both the private and the social security pension fund systems must be viewed within the context of the overall retirement income support system for the aged. The CPP and the QPP, together with the Old Age Security (OAS) program and the Guaranteed Annual Income Supplement (GIS), represent the public sector portion of Canada's pension and social security system.[2] In addition to the privately-sponsored employer pension plans, there is a large amount of savings locked away under the umbrella of a variety of Registered Retirement Savings Plans, which can be characterized as self-administered pension plans.

The CPP and QPP are social insurance plans which gear their benefits to the earnings-related contributions of both employees and employers. The CPP and QPP contributions are compulsory, cover nearly all employed and self-employed individuals, and both plans require no government contributions or subsidies. The retirement benefits are based on work-related contributions, although widows, widowers, orphans and disabled persons are also protected under the plan. The CPP is only partially funded and, in a sense, can be described as falling somewhere between a pay-as-you-go funding scheme and a fully-funded system.

Laurence E. Coward of William M. Mercer Ltd. has predicted that the changes affecting the private pensions plans will occur in areas where there is public dissatisfaction: "Whether as a result of pressure from the public or provincial legislation, private pension plans will almost certainly be improved in the future as regards to vesting of pensions for employees who leave, benefits for survivors, and adjustments for inflation."[3]

In the preparation of this chapter, which involved a review of appropriate literature as well as discussions with professionals in the industry, it became clear that substantial change was imminent.[4] But the problem of inflation, and the erosion of the purchasing power of private pension benefits, is a difficult one to resolve. There have been a number of proposals circulated concerning how to deal with the indexing problem. One of them involves the government of Canada in sponsoring an insurance plan for private pension funds in order to insulate them from unexpected increases in inflation. In an alternative plan, the government of Canada would provide real purchasing power bonds which the pension funds could hold in their portfolios.[5]

113

The Royal Commission on the Status of Pensions in Ontario recommends that private pensions be indexed by allowing pensioners to claim tax credits up to a certain maximum, which would transfer the cost of indexing to other taxpayers. A select committee of the Ontario legislature reviewed the indexing proposal and recommended inflation protection based on the excess interest rate approach — that is, the pension benefit would be increased each year by the additional interest earned on a pension fund or designated portfolio in excess of a specified rate.

In order for private pension plans to offer inflation-protected benefits, they in turn must have access to assets that are equally inflation-protected. The problem with most indexing schemes is that the institution that is designated to accept the inflation risk is always the federal government. That is, if inflation accelerates, the insuring group or the source of the indexing of last resort will be the federal government. This creates a potentially serious financing problem for the Ottawa government.

Overlaying the problem of private pension benefits in an inflationary environment is an additional concern over equity. Privately-sponsored pension plans cover only a part of the work force, and their membership is skewed towards both high wage earners and those who work for large, financially-secure firms. As a result, the income distribution effects associated with Ottawa's accepting the inflation indexing risk for private pension plans appear inequitable, unless other measures are introduced to compensate those who are not covered by private pension plans.

In the absence of devices that would shift the inflation risk to government, most employers would obviously prefer to continue the present practice of ad hoc benefit adjustments, rather than have their responsibilities legislated in this regard. Short of eliminating inflation, there seems to be no easy solution which will satisfy both employers concerned with the solvency of pension plans under their management and employees concerned with the purchasing power of pension benefits. In effect, ad hoc adjustments to benefits can be viewed as passing on some of the unexpected excess interest earned as interest rates adjust to higher inflation.

Of course, a portion of the pensioner's income, that which flows from the OAS, GIS, CPP and QPP, is completely indexed. Nevertheless, there is some concern in this area as well. This centres on the funding arrangements for the CPP. Under present trends, the CPP is rapidly becoming a pure pay-as-you-go system. This may or

114

may not be desirable, but from the perspective of the capital markets, such a development would be important.

All of these concerns have emerged at a time when the Canadian economy and its capital markets are under pressure. High inflation, slow economic growth, high unemployment and an uncertain government policy stance are the dominant features of the current picture. Since the impact of demographic changes, which are known with somewhat more certainty, is widely expected to create problems for both the private and public pension industry, the additional effects of the current economic situation on the capital markets are a matter of serious concern. Private pension funds in the 1980s may, therefore, experience the same difficulties in generating adequate real rates of return to their investments that occurred during the 1970s.

The Rate of Return Problem for Private Pension Plans

There are basically two different kinds of private pension plans: defined contribution plans and defined benefit plans. In the former case, employers and employees pay a proportion of the wage or salary into a fund. Upon retirement, the accumulated capital is used to purchase an annuity. Defined benefit systems are more popular. Under these plans, the employer promises to pay the worker retirement benefits which are calculated as a fixed percentage of the employee's salary, based upon the number of years of service. Defined benefit plans differ depending upon how benefits are calculated. There are benefits based on the average salary of the last five years, the final year's salary, or the highest salary level.

The various types of plans offer different protection against inflation in the pre-retirement years. The final and best average plans, which are widely used in the public sector, pay benefits according to a service-determined ratio of the pension base. The base is determined by earnings in the employee's best year, or years, of service. Since wages and salaries rise more or less proportionately with the price level, the employee's pension at the point of retirement (i.e., the replacement ratio) has been adjusted reasonably well for inflation. But, without indexing, the real value of the pension benefit declines during retirement. With few exceptions, only public sector pensions are indexed during the retirement years, and this applies to only two-thirds of public sector employees. In the private sector, fewer than 5 per cent of pension plan members enjoy indexed pensions, and typically this involves less than full indexation.

115

There exists a similar concern with guaranteeing real rates of return for equity portfolios. Many studies undertaken in Canada and the U.S. point to a consistent and negative correlation between inflation and real returns on equities. The data presented in Table 8-1, taken from a study published by James Pesando, point to five research studies which support this empirical conclusion. On the basis of these studies, it appears that equities are simply not a reliable hedge against inflation. And, again, although bond yields move up with increases in expected inflation, the very process of purchasing higher-yielding bond assets can force capital losses on the existing bonds in the portfolios. What is needed is some real protection for the portfolio, some form of indexed bonds or some way of making up a shortfall from nominal returns that are available in the market.

Some have suggested that the federal government should issue indexed bonds and have argued that private borrowers may follow suit. This suggestion involves numerous difficulties and would have a large, and perhaps unpredictable, impact on the capital markets. What will be

TABLE 8-1
THE IMPACT OF INFLATION ON THE REAL RETURNS
TO COMMON STOCKS—US AND CANADIAN EVIDENCE

Investigator (Year)	Data and Sample Period	Conclusions
Body (1976)	Monthly, quarterly and annual US data, 1953-72	Both expected and unexpected inflation depress real returns.
Branch (1975)	Annual data, 22 countries, 1953-69	Realized inflation depresses real returns.
Lintner (1973)	Annual US data, 1900-71	Realized inflation depresses real returns.
Nelson (1976)	Monthly US data, 1953-74	Both expected and unexpected inflation depress real returns.
Pesando & Rea (1976)	Quarterly Canadian data, 1957-73	Both expected and unexpected inflation depress real returns.

Source: This summary was presented in a survey study by Pesando. See James E. Pesando, *The Impact of Inflation on Financial Markets in Canada* (Montreal: C.D. Howe Research Institute, 1977), pp. 22, 37.

the impact on private borrowers? Would they have to imitate the federal government? If so, could they afford the risk? Who or what institutions should have access to these bonds? What volume of indexed bonds is called for? Is this scheme inflationary? Who gains and who loses from such a scheme? There are so many unknowns, some of them problematic, and there will likely be so much opposition, that the whole idea seems to have little chance of being implemented.

An alternative that has been suggested is that the federal government establish an insurance fund which would cover shortfalls in nominal returns to pension funds that are attributable to inflation. The private pension plans would pay an insurance premium to gain access to the insurance coverage. The insurance plan would end up transferring funds to the pension plans when inflation is higher than the long-term expected norm, and will be a net receiver of funds from the pension plans when inflation is below the long-term norm. Because the risk of inflation is not subject to actuarial calculations, private enterprise would not provide such insurance. The government can do it because of its ability to meet an unanticipated liquidity drain. There are a series of hazards in the approach which are not explored here. The insurance fund may or may not be a likely candidate for dealing with the problem; at the moment it does not appear to be popular in policy-making circles.

It is clear that governments will be irresistibly drawn into the issue. The real question is whether a rational and equitable umbrella scheme can be designed and implemented, or whether government involvement will be entirely ad hoc, possibly at the level of dealing with only the serious cases of old age poverty through traditional welfare programs. The above two somewhat exotic plans are possible candidates for a unified programmatic approach. A more mundane, and to some a more sensible, alternative is to increase the role of the CPP.

In a lengthy study released in late 1979, the Economic Council of Canada raised the issue of adequacy of the coverage of the CPP and considered the notion of expanding it to provide a retirement income replacement rate of 50 per cent of average industrial earnings, instead of the present target of 25 per cent. The council also considered the possibility of establishing a fully-funded supplement to the CPP, from which employers could contract out if their private plans provided benefits at least equal to the public plan. The supplement would provide a pension equal to 25 per cent of the average wage on top of the present 25 per cent maximum. But the council withheld approval of either an expanded CPP or a supplemental plan, because both would increase government intervention in the retirement field and might reduce incentives for improvement of private pension plans. Instead, the council proposed "certain more limited steps" to improve private plans "while urging employers and labour to expand coverage of the 'private' system without delay."[6]

Financing Social Security Plans

Concerns about financing private pension plans carry over into the social security system. Here, however, a new wrinkle emerges, since some people argue that government-run pension plans need not, and perhaps should not, be fully funded. At the other extreme, there are those who argue that the social insurance programs are, in many ways, comparable to private plans, and that they require actuarial studies and long-range cost estimates in order to assure one and all that the plans are actuarially sound.

As William M. Mercer Ltd. has noted in its March 1978 monthly letter, concerns over the solvency of the CPP are exaggerated.[7] When the CPP was being designed back in 1964, all of the earlier projections indicated that

> between 1980 and 1985 benefits would exceed contributions, that securities would have to start being liquidated between 1985 and 1990, and that the fund would be exhausted somewhere between 1996 and 2004. In other words, the CPP is behaving exactly as predicted in 1964. It was clearly anticipated that contributions would have to be raised as the plan matured. Certainly no one should complain that the government misled anyone or that the current position is a surprise.[8]

Although the CPP and QPP are contributory plans, they are not fully funded, unlike employer-sponsored plans. According to law, all private pension plans must take in sufficient contributions to meet not only current pension obligations but also future obligations, as amortized over a fifteen-year period. The funding of private pension plans in this manner guarantees the security of such plans even if the companies that sponsor them go out of business. The law does not apply to public plans or to the federal government civil service plans, since it is presumed that the Canadian government cannot go out of business.

If the CPP fund was entirely managed on a private actuarial basis, its savings would have to be invested in the Canadian equity and bond markets and in foreign securities. If the annual flow of new contributions (about $6 billion in 1978) was to be invested in the

118

private market, for example, it would more than swallow up the flow of the new bond and stock issues in Canada, which in 1977 amounted to about $2 billion. Thus, the bulk of these new funds would quickly flow towards the purchases of existing securities, and in very short order the CPP would end up being the majority stockholder in many Canadian private institutions. Such possibilities are likely to be viewed as undesirable by a large segment of the population. As will be seen later in this chapter, if the CPP fund was sufficient in size to match its theoretical "unfunded liability," then these problems would be far greater than they are.

The CPP is fairly close to becoming a pay-as-you-go system. The current contributions are paying benefits to the current generation of retirees. The CPP has built up a fund in excess of $12 billion, and the QPP fund has risen to about $5 billion since its start-up. But it is projected that by 1983 outflows from the CPP fund will exceed inflows, and the fund, while growing, will expand at a slower rate. Figures relating to the future trends in the CPP fund are presented in a later section of this chapter.

As shown in Table 8-2, the CPP and QPP funds hold rather different

TABLE 8-2
PUBLIC AND PRIVATE PENSION PLAN INVESTMENTS, END OF 1976
(% Distribution)

Type of Plan & Total Assets	Claims on Govts	Corp. Bonds	Corp. Equities	Mort-gages	Other[1]
Canada Pension Plan					
$10.9 billion	100	0	0	0	0
Quebec Pension Plan					
$4.0 billion	62	10	15	5	8
Public employer plans					
$35.7 billion	81	5	5	6	4
Private employer plans					
$18.9 billion	15	21	27	25	13
RRSPs					
$7.5 billion	10	10	15	59	6
All plans					
$77.1 billion	59	9	11	15	6

Note: [1]Includes cash, money market paper, real estate and foreign securities.

Source: Task Force on Retirement Income Policy to the Government of Canada, *The Retirement Income System in Canada: Problems and Alternative Policies for Reform* (Ottawa: Canadian Government Publishing Centre, 1980), vol. 1, p. 78.

assets in their portfolios. The QPP funds are invested in a wider range of assets, with about $2.7 billion in Quebec provincial or provincially-backed bonds in 1976. Many observers have noted that Quebec's dependence on the QPP has increased as foreign lenders have become more hesitant due to the political situation in that province. In the case of the CPP, its funds have been invested in 20-year provincial bonds at lower than their market interest rates. As well, the nine participating provinces have been permitted to borrow back the interest owing on their primary borrowings. This has been a fiscal boon to the provinces. Clearly, the provinces will face new financing challenges after 1984 when the CPP may have to begin calling in their loans. Of course, contribution rates may be adjusted so that the size of the reserve fund increases.

The provincial governments have benefited extraordinarily because of their access to CPP funds. In the five years ended March 31, 1978, for example, the provinces participating in the CPP raised for themselves, and for their provincially-guaranteed entities, a total of $18 billion in net new financing, of which CPP supplied $6.9 billion or about 38 per cent.[9] The provinces have been able to raise money at a lower borrowing rate through the CPP than through their securities floated in the marketplace. For example, a review completed in 1975 showed that on average a yield differential in the cost of borrowing funds for the provinces ranged from a low of 112 basis points for Ontario to a high of 165 basis points for British Columbia on issues maturing twenty-five years into the future.[10] Most people simply are not aware of how important CPP loans are to provincial finances.

As well, the financing problem for the CPP has come sharply into focus because of demographic studies which indicate that the average age of Canada's population will rise significantly between the late 1970s and the year 2000. The prospective aging of the population will either necessitate sharp increases in the CPP contribution rates to maintain the current relative levels of benefits, or the use of other sources of tax revenue for benefits.

There is a more subtle aspect to the issue of social security funding which has to do with the impact on private earnings and the rate of national capital accumulation. In the U.S. and Canada, several prominent economists have warned that public pension plans may be having a substantial negative impact on the rate of private savings. Indeed, it has been argued that the pay-as-you-go social insurance system has had a significant negative impact on the level of private savings and that, as a result of this effect, the U.S. social security system has caused a substantial reduction in the nation's stock of physical capital and hence its production capacity.

A version of this argument has also surfaced in Canada, subject to the qualification that the CPP is partially funded. Thus the CPP is not as close to a pure pay-as-you-go system as is the U.S. social security system, though it surely is moving in that direction. A pure pay-as-you-go financing system would have the contributions to the plan immediately distributed as benefits rather than accumulated within a fund. To the extent that contributors consider such benefits to be compulsory savings, they may tend to reduce their personal savings. Private pension funds, or fully-vested public employer-sponsored pension plans, must build up an adequate reserve fund, and, in principle, such financing arrangements need not have a negative effect on national savings.

It is important to realize that when the CPP began in 1966, the personal savings rate was about 6 per cent. The rate drifted slightly downwards until the early 1970s and then began to climb; it has exceeded 10 per cent in some recent years. Yet Canada's aggregate savings or investment to GNP ratio has remained relatively constant over the past twenty-five years. In general, it is not clear that the CPP plan has had a negative effect on other forms of saving.

The Social Security System and its Impact on National Savings

According to the statistics published in Statistics Canada's *National Income and Expenditure Accounts*, social security savings — that is, the difference between the total revenues generated by the CPP and QPP and their total outlays — have become an important source of total government savings. In 1978, all levels of government dissaved at a $5.1 billion rate. But the deficit was entirely in the federal government's budget ($10.7 billion). The provinces, local governments and hospitals together generated a surplus of about $3 billion. The social security system (i.e., the CPP and QPP) generated a surplus of $2.5 billion. Table 8-3 shows historical figures back to 1968 which indicate that social security has been consistently important in terms of government savings. If social security savings were not available for government financing and not identified as part of government savings, as they are in this table, the total government deficit would have been 50 per cent higher in 1978.

The figures presented in Table 8-4 provide some indication of the importance of social security savings relative to total gross savings in

TABLE 8-3
SOCIAL SECURITY SAVINGS AND GOVERNMENT SAVINGS IN
CANADA, 1968-78
($ millions)

Year	Total Revenues CPP & QPP	Total Expen. CPP & QPP	Social Security Savings	Total Govt Savings[1]	Social Security Savings as a % of Govt Savings
1968	1,040	37	1,003	3,030	33.1%
1969	1,190	77	1,113	4,183	26.6
1970	1,327	134	1,193	3,327	35.8
1971	1,478	200	1,278	2,510	50.9
1972	1,657	282	1,375	2,570	53.5
1973	1,875	403	1,472	3,832	38.4
1974	2,318	538	1,780	6,122	29.1
1975	2,780	773	2,003	−220	Govt saving neg.
1976	3,282	1,097	2,183	92	Govt saving neg.
1977	3,686	1,427	2,259	−2,329	Govt saving neg.
1978	4,231	1,782	2,449	−5,077	Govt saving neg.

Note: [1]Includes federal, provincial and local governments and hospital savings plus CPP and QPP savings shown here.

Source: Statistics Canada, *National Income and Expenditure Accounts,* First Quarter 1971 and Second Quarter 1979.

Canada since 1972. The net saving of the CPP and QPP accounted for approximately 5 per cent of total gross savings in the years shown. This is a substantial amount of money, and its future savings effect is important since these savings flows are expected to moderate in the 1980s.

Table 8-5 illustrates how the CPP fund may behave between 1978 and 2050 under a series of different assumptions. The benefit payout and administrative expense costs of the CPP are assumed to be the same in all three of the simulations considered. The primary assumption utilized for the Fund A calculations is that the contribution rate will remain fixed at 3.6 per cent. Under this assumption, the CPP fund reaches its maximum level in 1990 at $34.2 billion. After that date, the fund starts to contract and becomes completely exhausted by the year 2003. When the fund rises, savings are generated. When it falls, savings turn negative.

Fund B is identical to Fund A during its initial phase. But the net cash flow to the provinces is not permitted to become negative; instead the contribution rate of the members is increased to a level that matches current expenditures (Benefits and Expenses). Under Fund B's

122

TABLE 8-4
SOURCES OF GROSS SAVINGS IN CANADA, SELECTED YEARS, 1972-78
($ millions and/or % of Total Savings)

	1972		1975		1978	
	$	%	$	%	$	%
Net saving:						
Persons and unincorporated business[1]	5,015	21.4	12,139	30.2	16,042	30.6
Corporate and government business enterprise[2]	3,538	15.1	5,078	12.7	9,992	19.0
Undistributed profits of corporations	4,154	17.7	7,790	19.4	13,074	24.4
Government	2,570	11.0	−220	−0.5	−5,077	−9.6
CPP & QPP	1,375	5.9	2,003	5.0	2,449	4.7
Non-residents	667	2.8	5,252	13.1	5,679	10.8
Capital consumption allowances[3]	11,474	49.0	18,270	45.6	25,146	48.0
Total gross savings[4]	23,405		40,105		52,420	
Personal savings ratios[5]		7.4		10.9		10.9

Notes: [1] Excludes an adjustment on grain transactions.
[2] Includes undistributed corporation profits, undistributed profits of government enterprise, capital assistance and inventory valuation adjustment.
[3] Possibly this item could be included with corporate saving.
[4] The final total includes a residual error term and an adjustment for grain transactions.
[5] The ratio of personal savings to personal disposable income.

Source: Statistics Canada, *National Income and Expenditure Accounts,* First Quarter 1971 and Second Quarter 1979.

assumptions, interest payments by the provinces to the fund would never be used for purposes of expenditures, and thus would be continuously returnable to the provinces in the form of new loans. These assumptions result in an ever-growing fund.

Fund C is a pure pay-as-you-go option. The contribution rate would increase sufficiently so that the contributions of members plus interest earnings would exactly equal expenditures on a current basis. On this basis, the loans made to the provinces are, in effect, renewed for perpetuity. This is in contrast to the Fund B assumptions, where the interest payments by the provinces to the fund are not required for purposes of paying benefits and expenses.

In other words, Fund A shows the expected progress of the fund if there were absolutely no changes in benefits or contribution rates until

TABLE 8-5
CPP RESERVE FUND: THREE ALTERNATIVE SCENARIOS
PRESENTED BY THE DEPARTMENT OF INSURANCE[1]

Calendar Year	Benefits and Expenses	Contribu- tion Rate	Contri- butions	Cash Flow to Provinces	Fund at End of Year
		FUND A 3.6% Contribution Rate			
1978	1,386		2,096	710	14.3
1979	1,752		2,376	625	16.1
1980	2,152		2,674	522	17.9
1981	2,553		2,992	439	19.8
1982	2,993		3,323	330	21.7
1983	3,427		3,666	238	23.7
1984	3,901		4,016	116	25.6
1985	4,415		4,372	−43	27.5
1986	5,000		4,702	−299	29.3
1987	5,630		5,038	−591	30.9
1990	7,794		6,142	−1,652	34.2
1995	12,297		8,579	−3,718	32.1
2000[2]	18,416		11,997	−6,418	14.5
		FUND B Cash Flow to Provinces Decreases Until Zero			
1978	1,386	3.60	2,096	710	14.3
1979	1,752	3.60	2,376	625	16.1
1980	2,152	3.60	2,674	522	17.9
1981	2,553	3.60	2,992	439	19.8
1982	2,993	3.60	3,323	330	21.7
1983	3,427	3.60	3,666	238	23.7
1984	3,901	3.60	4,016	116	25.6
1985	4,415	3.64	4,415	0	27.6
1986	5,000	3.83	5,000	0	29.7
1987	5,630	4.02	5,630	0	31.9
1990	7,794	4.57	7,794	0	39.5
1995	12,297	5.16	12,297	0	55.5
2000	18,416	5.53	18,416	0	76.7
2005	26,766	5.74	26,766	0	105.1
2010	39,850	6.20	39,850	0	144.0
2025	135,629	8.62	135,629	0	370.5
2030	193,314	9.09	193,314	0	507.6
2050	636,210	8.76	636,210	0	1,788.5

TABLE 8-5 continued

Calendar Year	Benefits and Expenses	Contribution Rate	Contributions	Cash Flow to Provinces	Fund at End of Year
		FUND C			
	Cash Flow to Provinces Decreases Until Negative and Equal to Interest on Fund				
1978	1,386	3.60	2,096	710	14.3
1979	1,752	3.60	2,376	625	16.1
1980	2,152	3.60	2,674	522	17.9
1981	2,553	3.60	2,992	439	19.8
1982	2,993	3.60	3,323	330	21.7
1983	3,427	3.60	3,666	238	23.7
1984	3,901	3.60	4,016	116	25.6
1985	4,415	3.60	4,372	−43	27.5
1986	5,000	3.60	4,702	−299	29.3
1987	5,630	3.60	5,038	−591	30.9
1990	7,794	3.60	6,142	−1,652	34.2
1995	12,297	4.13	9,847	−2,451	34.7
2000	18,416	4.84	16,146	−2,270	34.7
2005	26,766	5.26	24,512	−2,255	34.7
2010	39,850	5.85	37,596	−2,255	34.7
2025	135,629	8.48	133,374	−2,255	34.7
2030	193,314	8.98	191,060	−2,255	34.7
2050	636,210	8.73	633,955	−2,255	34.7

Notes: [1]Fund in billions of dollars, other dollar figures in millions, contribution rate as per cent of contributory earnings.

[2]Fund would become exhausted in 2003, and contribution rate would have to rise to "Fund B" level or other revenue found.

Source: Department of Insurance, Canada Pension Plan Statutory Actuarial Report No. 6 as at December 31, 1977.

the fund became exhausted in 2003. As the federal Department of Insurance notes, it is unlikely that the CPP contingency fund would be allowed to shrink in this way, and then become fully exhausted. The other two alternatives, Funds B and C, are more plausible. The real question is: Will the CPP become a pure pay-as-you-go system after 1995, as envisioned in the Fund C calculations, or will the size of the reserve fund be encouraged to grow over time?

TABLE 8-6
THE DEPARTMENT OF INSURANCE ESTIMATE OF THE
UNFUNDED LIABILITY OF THE CPP, 1977

Case Assumptions	Increase in CPI	Increase in Earnings	Interest on New Investments 1978	Interest on New Investments 1983 & Later	Entry-Age-Normal Contribution Rate	1977 Unfunded Liability
	%	%	%	%	%	$b
Fund A	3.5	5.5	9.4	6.5	8.04	81.3
Fund B	4.0	5.5	9.4	6.5	8.48	85.4
Fund C	3.5	5.5	9.4	6.0	9.38	84.4

Source: Department of Insurance, Canada Pension Plan Statutory Actuarial Report No. 6 as at December 31, 1977.

It is interesting to note that for the 1980s, the forecasting period for this study, changes in the size of the fund are not very dramatic under any of the simulations. In all three cases, the rate of increase in the size of the fund moderates, which implies that the CPP will provide a smaller (but positive) flow of savings to the national economy.

Finally, in Table 8-6 the Department of Insurance provides a hypothetical estimate of the amount of unfunded liability due to the CPP. The unfunded liability is the amount of money that would have to be credited to the CPP account in 1978, and invested at the rates assumed applicable to new investments at that time, so that the CPP was fully funded as an actuarially sound, private pension plan. Obviously, this calculation is sensitive to the amount of interest that the fund earns and to the different contribution rate assumptions. The main point to be highlighted is that the size of this hypothetical, unfunded liability is enormous, and that any attempt to place the CPP on a private, actuarially sound basis would require a tremendous flow of new savings into the CPP, and very high contribution rates.

The QPP is managed by the Caisse de Dépôt et Placement du Québec and it invests in a wider range of securities than the CPP. The CPP is virtually all invested in provincial government, non-negotiable securities. In contrast, the QPP held 15 per cent of its portfolio in equities, 5 per cent in mortgages and 10 per cent in corporation bonds at the end of 1976. The QPP also has an unfunded liability.

It should be noted again that an unfunded liability in a government social security plan is not necessarily a bad thing. Some argue that these plans should be run on a pay-as-you-go basis. As illustrated above, the CPP is moving in this direction. Thus it will stop being a source of savings.

The size of the theoretical, unfunded liability for the CPP/QPP is so big that it is unlikely the capital market would be able to absorb the funds if they were actually generated. While it is true that some of the funds that would be raised by the social security system would result in declines in other forms of savings, we do not think that this replacement effect would be sufficient. Furthermore, the scale of the effective tax hikes (or increase in contribution rates) necessary for full funding would be so deflationary on the real economy that it is unlikely to be seriously considered. In fact, others who have studied the question, including some in the actuarial field, do not appear to take the full-funding option for the social security system very seriously.

Growth Prospects for the Private and Social Security Pension Plans

This section attempts to tie together some of the implications of the preceding discussion for the capital markets in general. The institutional and legislative framework that will shape the pension fund industry is, at present, in a state of flux. Most experts argue that some form of liberalized vesting arrangements and some form of mandatory indexing of private pension bencfits will emerge in the 1980s. Moreover, it may very well be that the importance of the CPP/QPP may increase in the 1980s. Will such developments be positive or negative from the viewpoint of the pension fund industry?

More liberalized private plan vesting arrangements and improvements in the pensioner's protection against inflation together will imply increases in the flow of contributions into pension funds. This could involve increases in employee or employer contribution rates, possibly augmented by funds channeled through federal government budgets. The latter may take the form of the provision of some type of indexed bond that could be purchased by pension funds, or alternatively, some form of guarantee which would permit the pension fund industry to realize the real rates of return consistent with the form of indexing chosen.

Even without such new arrangements, the flow of funds into private pensions will increase more rapidly than in the past due to the aging of the population. An individual worker's real wage tends to rise due to seniority and experience as he moves through his working years, giving him rates of wage growth higher than the average for the economy as he approaches the peak of his life cycle of earnings. With contributions in most plans rising proportionately with wages, an aging of the population means a step-up in the total level of contributions. As well, employers' contributions to pension plans rise as the workers get closer to retirement. The average age of Canada's work force is expected to increase by about 5 years over the 1980s. Thus, the aging of the population is likely to have a sizeable impact on pension funds even if there is little change in the quality of benefits.

But there are also a number of factors which must be regarded as negative for the prospects of this industry. It seems clear that some further encroachment of the social security system (the CPP and QPP) on the private pension market is quite possible. Moreover, the private pension industry has already experienced rapid growth, in part because it has completely penetrated the public employment sector of the labour force. This sector is expected to grow less rapidly than the private sector labour force in the 1980s. Demographic studies also suggest that the overall growth of the Canadian labour force is starting to moderate, a trend that is not expected to reverse until the 1990s. Thus, some of the momentum of past growth will be lost, though this too may be offset by some increase in private sector coverage.

The net effect of the positive and negative factors that will influence private pension fund asset growth is likely to be positive. Historical trends indicate an asset/GNP elasticity for pension funds significantly greater than unity between 1961 and 1978.[11] Our analysis suggests that this relation, in which private pension funds grow more rapidly than GNP, will continue.

This view is consistent with the conclusion reached in a recently published study of pensions by the Economic Council of Canada. "With the aging of the population that is foreseen and the pressure to improve benefits . . . it seems very likely that pension funds will not only grow rather rapidly in the future, but that they will grow more rapidly than other long-term saving institutions."[12]

The Social Security/Private Sector Mix

Many prominent study groups have suggested that the mix of pension coverage between the social security system (the CPP and QPP) and the private sector should shift in the 1980s. It is useful in this regard to consider the recommendations for such expanded coverage made by the Quebec Confirentes report, the report of the Economic Council of Canada referred to above, and the report of the Senate Committee, chaired by Senator Croll, entitled "Retirement Without Tears."

The January 1980 issue of *The Mercer Bulletin* summarized these recommendations as follows:

> The Croll Committee has proposed a vast expansion of the Canada and Quebec Pension Plans. The contributions would rise from the present 1.8% each from employers and employees to 4% each in two years and the pensionable earnings (YMPE) would rise to 1.5 times the average industrial wage. The report states that this would allow the pensions to be roughly doubled. . . . The Confirentes Report did not go quite so far. It proposed that the contributions should be raised to 3.4% over a five-year period and that a schedule of future increases in contributions be written into the Act, as in the United States. The pension would be doubled for those earning less than half the YMPE and raised by 50% for those at the maximum. . . . The Economic Council takes an entirely different position, proposing that the contributions to the CPP/QPP be increased moderately every few years but without significant change in the benefits. Instead, any increase in the basic income of the elderly should come from discretionary changes in the Guaranteed Income Supplement.[13]

What happens to the private pension industry will obviously be very much affected by the decisions made with regard to the CPP/QPP. It is very difficult to predict whether Ottawa will choose to legislate and provide incentives leading to an improvement in the quality of private pension benefits, or whether it will choose to expand the role of the social security system. Some of both may be the most likely outcome. However, if the expansion of the CPP/QPP predominates in the government's solution to the pension problem, forecasts for growth in the private pension industry will have to be scaled down.

One thing that is reasonable to predict, however, is considerable delay before the relevant decisions are taken and implemented. To the degree that decisions about changing the CPP contribution rates are related to the CPP funding issue, a full decade's delay is possible. The indexing of private pension benefits is a more pressing issue, but an overall integrated solution to it is still so complex that the design of a program could still take years, particularly in the current political environment. Some ad hoc interim measures may be forthcoming in the meantime.

Assets Available to Private Pension Plans

This capital market analysis suggested that several important developments may shift private portfolio opportunities away from their present distributions. For example, there is the expected secular slowdown in Canada's housing industry, which will stem out of a series of demographic trends now under way. The moderation of new housing activity could extend until the mid-1990s in Canada, and this implies a moderation in the growth of the stock of residential mortgages outstanding.

Several alternatives to these expected housing trends are possible, but they cannot be taken too seriously in terms of the implications for the mortgage industry. If housing inflation outpaces the general rate of inflation, as was the case in the past, then the financing needs for new and existing housing units will rise more rapidly. As well, if a mortgage payment deductibility scheme is introduced in the 1980s, this could give a temporary boost to the demand for new housing, since it would result in a decline in the relative (after-tax) price of houses. But this effect would be temporary: housing prices would tend to rise at a faster pace until a new equilibrium level of housing inflation was restored.

This chapter identified the likelihood that an important source of provincial finance will dry up as the growth in CPP and QPP funds slows in the 1980s. The CPP fund could become a pure pay-as-you-go plan by the early 1990s. This ''squeeze-out'' effect implies that provincial financing will shift back more heavily either into long-term domestic markets or into the external markets. The provinces and their agencies have relied heavily on CPP and QPP for direct finance, and this source will likely diminish in the 1980s.

In terms of the spending orientation of the economy, the projected bulge of business energy investment in the decade of the 1980s is important. This type of economic growth is very different from the surge in consumer spending associated with the 1960s and the first half of the 1970s. Which institutions will finance the bulk of the large wave of business and energy-oriented investment?

This issue must be placed in the perspective of our most likely inflation projection, which suggests that inflation will remain high through most of the decade. This proposition carries with it the probability that the long-term corporate bond market will continue to languish relative to the demand for funds by corporations. High inflation will continue to be associated with a relative shortening of the term structure of corporate and government debt, and a further backing out of the debt markets by corporations into the banks and near banks (spurred on by the new Canadian Bank Act) will occur.

One related development which emerged in the 1970s and partly accounted for the relative drying up of the new issue corporate bond market in Canada was the emergence of "after tax" corporate financing. This allowed industrial corporations in Canada to bypass the open markets and shift a greater proportion of their long-term financing directly to chartered banks. While the tax legislation that allowed this trend to develop has been rescinded for large corporations, similar legislation could be reintroduced in the future in response to the continuing pressures of high inflation and high interest rates. In other words, this is one additional possible reason for expecting the relative supply of corporate financial instruments available for purchase by the pension fund industry to be limited.

To place these trends in the perspective of the make-up of portfolios, consider the figures in Table 8-7 which set out the percentage distribution of trusteed pension fund assets between 1960 and 1977. The table provides market value measures of asset holdings, though the observations we draw at this point seem to relate relatively equally to either market or book values.

Trusteed pension plans in 1961 held 71.1 per cent of their assets in bonds (very heavily invested in provincial governments), about 13 per cent of their portfolio in equities, and about 8.3 per cent in mortgages. After social security was introduced in the mid-1960s, trusteed pension plans reduced their relative holdings in provincial and municipal securities.

Two factors seem to have been at work in altering these relative asset distributions. Many provincial governments have taken over the direct financing of municipal activities since the 1960s, and in turn the provinces have shifted their borrowing heavily into the social security system by issuing non-negotiable bonds.

The mortgage asset portion of portfolios rose from 8.3 per cent in 1961 to 13.6 per cent in 1977, a trend which seems to parallel the extensive new housing activity that occurred in the 1960s and the early 1970s. Further, as the share of the provincial and municipal bonds declined in the private pension plan portfolios, equities took their place. Finally, with rising inflation, short-term investments rose as a proportion of the total assets held by the private pension plans between the early 1960s and the late 1970s.

Based on this brief review of trusteed pension plan portfolios and a shift of projected capital market developments, the following portfolio shifts could occur in the 1980s:

• Private pension fund portfolios may, in the late 1980s, increase their relative holdings of the provincial government and agency bonds compared with their positions in the late 1970s.

131

TABLE 8-7
SUMMARY OF ASSET DISTRIBUTION OF TRUSTEED PENSION FUNDS, SELECTED YEARS, 1960-77
($ millions)

	1961		1965		1970		1977	
	$	%	$	%	$	%	$	%
Investment in pooled pension funds	135	3.3	456	6.8	767	7.3	1,737	5.8
Investment in mutual funds	41	1.0	40	0.6	65	0.6	43	0.1
Investment in segregated funds	—	—	—	—	—	—	468	1.6
Bonds:								
Government of Canada	560	13.7	473	7.0	407	3.9	1,119	3.8
Provincial governments	1,270	31.1	1,963	29.2	2,747	26.0	7,589	25.7
Municipal, school boards, etc.	419	10.3	619	9.2	641	6.1	1,093	3.7
Other Canadian	647	15.8	965	14.4	1,349	12.8	4,270	14.5
Non-Canadian	9	0.2	4	0.1	10	0.1	10	—
Total	2,905	71.1	4,024	59.9	5,154	48.9	14,081	47.7
Stocks:								
Canadian, common	445	10.9	1,042	15.5	2,223	21.0	5,461	18.5
Canadian, preferred	17	0.4	29	0.5	67	0.6	59	0.2
Non-Canadian, common	67	1.7	223	3.3	541	5.1	892	3.0
Non-Canadian, preferred	—	—	1	—	9	0.1	3	—
Total	529	13.0	1,295	19.3	2,840	26.8	6,415	21.7

	1961		1965		1970		1977	
	$	%	$	%	$	%	$	%
Mortgages:								
Insured residential (NHA)	231	5.6	367	5.5	512	4.8	2,196	7.5
Conventional	110	2.7	252	3.7	496	4.7	1,806	6.1
Total	341	8.3	619	9.2	1,008	9.5	4,002	13.6
Real estate and lease-backs	33	0.8	44	0.6	48	0.5	202	0.7
Miscellaneous:								
Cash on hand	42	1.0	103	1.5	136	1.3	526	1.8
Guaranteed investment certificates	—	—	18	0.3	110	1.0	254	0.9
Short-term investments	—	—	32	0.5	278	2.6	1,213	4.1
Accrued interest and dividends receivable	36	0.9	55	0.8	90	0.8	305	1.0
Accounts receivable	21	0.5	32	0.5	75	0.7	289	1.0
Other assets	2	0.1	2	—	3	—	3	—
Total	101	2.5	242	3.6	692	6.4	2,590	8.8
Total assets	4,085	100.0	6,720	100.0	10,574	100.0	29,538	100.0

Source: Statistics Canada, *Trusteed Pension Plans Financial Statistics, 1977* (Cat. No. 74-201), p. 14.

- Private pension funds will decrease their holdings of residential mortgages as a proportion of their total assets.
- Since inflation will remain high, short-term interest rates will also remain high and the short-term investment proportion of pension fund portfolios will likely move higher than the level reached in the late 1970s.
- The equity portion of portfolios will rise from the levels of the late 1970s in view of the high inflation outlook and the energy investment boom.
- Despite the higher rates of return on long-term bonds which are projected below, private pension funds will relatively avoid the long-term bond market for much of the next half-decade when inflation is projected to average about 10 per cent per annum. This will be partially offset by the amount of financing that will be needed for energy investment, which is so great that significant debt opportunities will appear.

Real Returns on Pension Fund Assets in the 1980s

Will the private pension funds be capable of generating more typically positive real rates of return on investment in the 1980s compared with their poor performance in the 1970s? The answer to this difficult question must be considered from several different perspectives.

If Canada's real economy grows at a significantly slower pace in the 1980s than during the 1960s and the first half of the 1970s, it stands to reason that the growth of its income components, real wages and interest, must similarly experience a moderation unless there occurs a substantial shift in the distribution of income.

But another aspect of this issue relates to this writer's expectation that the depressed levels of real interest rates that existed during much of the 1970s have already improved since 1979, and that real wages will tend to grow at below traditional rates of increase. Those who make actuarial calculations relating to the solvency of pension plans understand that it is the relative difference in the growth rates of real wages and real interest rates which affect the actuarial solvency calculations. In fact, real returns must be calculated for all portfolio assets, but in this discussion the analysis is limited to securities that carry a fixed coupon rate. Through much of the 1950s and 1960s the ex post real pre-tax returns to long-term investment in government securities averaged above 2 per cent, but that experience substantially deteriorated in the 1970s. The mechanics of that shift was the acceleration in the rate of inflation to levels at or above the prevailing returns on long-term government securities.

Through most of the 1970s, when pension fund portfolios were generating negative returns, real wages rose at abnormally high rates. In that environment, pension fund managers were unable to increase the market value of their portfolios in line with the near two-digit rate of inflation. As well, since their performance seemed so poor, pension funds were not in a position to do much more than offer the occasional amount of ad hoc inflation indexing for benefits.

The implications of some of the long-term capital market projections cited earlier are that real returns to investment are normalizing in the 1980s, but that real wage gains will remain somewhat depressed for the decade.

Conclusion

In this chapter we reviewed the empirical importance of pension fund savings to the Canadian capital markets. In addition, we considered the likely course of new legislation relating to vesting privileges, inflation indexing and the relative mix between the private system and the social security system.

These conclusions must be regarded as tentative since they could change depending upon the passage of new legislation relating to the competition for funds among financial institutions, and provincial and federal legislation concerning the private pension industry. Moreover, whether the CPP continues to move in the direction of a pure pay-as-you-go fund, or whether in the future its expansion will be based on a fully-funded investment portfolio, is also a very important consideration.

The conclusion reached by the Economic Council of Canada that in the 1980s the flow of savings through the private pension industry will exceed the rate of growth of total gross savings seems reasonable. This will occur despite the relative shift of labour from the highly pensionized government sector to the relatively under-penetrated private sector labour force. Essentially, the increase in the average age of Canada's population in the 1980s suggests that much more of Canada's total savings will go through the contractual private pension route.

Further, this analysis implies that the private pension industry will be shifting its assets more in the direction of provincial government bonds and shorter-term federal government bonds, and away from residential mortgage debt. We also suggest that the proportion of equities in pension fund portfolios will increase in the 1980s relative to levels of the previous decade.

These shifts will occur against a background of real returns on investment capital in the 1980s significantly stronger than those experienced in the 1970s. Whether these real returns will be held below the higher returns of the 1960s, or remain well above that level as they have in 1981 and 1982, remains an important question for the capital markets and the health of the economy.

Conclusion

The bulk of this study was completed at a time (1980-81) when the Canadian economy was experiencing a record series of difficulties, and when the prospects for the coming decade were very unclear. Consumer prices rose 12.5 per cent in Canada in 1981, and through all of 1980 and most of 1981 concerns over the size of the federal government deficit and the dispute between Ottawa and the provinces over energy prices and revenues (or rent) distribution, the constitutional issue, and high interest rates were threatening to keep the Canadian economy in a prolonged slump. By the end of 1981 the energy pricing dispute, the constitutional question, and the concern over the size of the federal government's borrowings had eased. But there was a growing realization that Canada's anti-inflation strategy, which was set in motion in 1975 when the rate of inflation was 9 per cent, had failed.

Back in 1975 the Canadian government introduced mandatory incomes controls under the Anti-Inflation Board (AIB) program, the Bank of Canada adopted its own version of monetarism, there was devaluation of the Canadian dollar, and the federal budget was shifted in the direction of restraint. With the exception of the termination of controls, which were removed in late 1978 and early 1979, the Canadian government has pursued roughly the same anti-inflation strategy since 1975, but nevertheless the mix of policies simply has not wrestled inflation down at all. The unpopular November 1981 federal budget shifted fiscal policy much more towards restraint, so that in 1982 both major policy levers were pointing in this direction. The 12.5 per cent rate of inflation in 1981 was fueled by very rapid oil price hikes, escalating food prices, weak productivity, and catch-up inflation momentum from wages and salaries. Speculation that Ottawa would introduce foreign exchange controls surfaced on several occasions in 1980, 1981 and 1982, as the Canadian dollar suffered in the foreign

137

exchange markets because of high U.S. interest rates. There was also considerable speculation in 1982 that Ottawa would reintroduce some form of prices and incomes control such as it had back in 1975.

Most medium- and long-term economic projections indicate that Canada will face the same kind of economic problems over the next decade as it experienced during the second half of the 1970s. In essence, high inflation, regional economic differences, current account deficits in the balance of payments, and relatively slow economic growth were, from the vantage point of early 1982, expected to continue to dominate national economic developments in Canada over the medium term.

Indeed, the energy issue, interest rates and inflation seem to be at the core of the capital market issues explored in this study. These issues all present a challenge in that, both separately and together, they impact on national economic priorities such as the development of capital infrastructure, equity in income distribution, and economic sovereignty. For example, the chapters dealing with energy financing and megaprojects (chapter 4), the mortgage market (chapter 7), and the westward shift of finance and industry (chapter 6) relate to the nation's economic development priorities. The chapters dealing with monetary policy, inflation and new initiatives in the financing of pension plans (chapters 2, 3 and 8) essentially touch on income distribution concerns, while the Canadianization discussion in chapter 5 examines the side effects of pursuing national economic sovereignty objectives.

The study began with a description of the institutions and markets which have a financial intermediary role in Canada and illustrated their interdependence using the example of a flow-of-funds statement. Obviously any serious disruption of these flows of funds, either between Canada and the rest of the world, or within the various regions of Canada, or indeed even between major financial sectors, must have an impact on the real economy through savings and investment decisions and then ultimately through production and employment changes. The restricted number of challenges for the capital markets discussed in the study tie into the question of financial blockages, which has spillovers into the real economy. In particular, the real spillover effects can be seen most directly in the chapters dealing with public and private pension funds, the financing of energy mega-projects, the Canadianization of industry, the mortgage market, and changes in the regional flows of funds to western Canada.

A flow-of-funds projection for the period 1981 to 1986 was reviewed with respect to the kind of capital market shifts that might

138

emerge. That projection suggested that the successful financing of future large-scale business investment will require a substantial decline in total government borrowing in order to free up funds for the corporate sector. We can also probably expect some diversion of funds away from mortgage finance into business investment. Foreign investors will also have to make an important portfolio shift, from essentially purchasing provincial government debt towards the purchase of corporate bonds and stocks. Concerns were expressed over the ease with which such massive realignments of savings flows could occur.

Chapter 2 dealt with the theoretical and practical interaction between inflation and the capital markets institutions. Most economists believe that inflation will continue to be an ongoing problem for the economies of the Western world in the 1980s and that therefore the financial institutions will continue to respond to the effects of inflation.

The financial markets effects stressed in the study are as follows:

- Inflation makes lenders unwilling to extend debt, especially because of the capital losses that lenders, both individuals and institutions, have suffered in recent years. Thus the terms of all fixed interest contracts have been and will continue to be short, including such important financing instruments as mortgages, corporation bonds and government bonds. This shortening of the term to maturity makes business and household investment planning extraordinarily difficult.

- The direct relationship between inflation rates and nominal interest rates is well understood: the interest rate is typically higher than the inflation rate, and real long-term yields fluctuate — at times they are positive such as during 1980 and 1981, and at times they are negative such as during much of the 1970s. Since higher inflation on its own has a higher variation around its mean (or a higher average rate of inflation has larger amplitudes in the inflation cycle), this on its own results in greater interest rate variability. Stated another way, the risk premium in interest rates has increased because of high inflation in the 1980s.

- The personal and corporation tax systems tend to distort savings and investment decisions because of inflation. High rates of inflation tend to depress real capital investment in Canada because the effective corporation income tax rate rises with every rise in the underlying rate of inflation.

- A major non-neutrality in the inflation process can be traced to the government attempts to curb inflation. Inflation results in tighter monetary and fiscal policies than would otherwise be the case, and through this mechanism slows real economic growth and creates higher unemployment. Moreover, when the rate of inflation in Canada is higher than in the U.S. (as it was in 1981), the Canadian government, which is often supporting the external value of the Canadian dollar, adopts higher interest rates in Canada to stabilize the downward pressure on the Canadian dollar.

- Inflation and the associated high interest rates result in businesses and consumers keeping a larger proportion of their transactions and precautionary balances in interest-bearing liquid assets. The practical value of using the narrowly defined money supply for central bank targeting purposes, defined as demand deposits that do not bear interest plus currency, loses credibility and value over time as inflation and interest rates move higher.

- Finally, it was argued that the drying up of the corporate bond market, in particular, has probably favoured the large banks at the expense of Canada's investment dealers. The banks now receive a form of corporate business which normally would have flowed out into open market financing, and this trend in fact concentrates the power of the banks even more within the financial system.

Chapter 3 considered the economic and financial ramifications for the Canadian economy stemming from the application of fairly restrictive monetary policies by the Bank of Canada and the U.S. Federal Reserve System since 1979. In Canada these practices resulted in monetary aggregate growth rates considerably below target levels in 1981, extraordinarily high nominal and real interest rates, a series of exchange rate/mortgage interest rate renewal crises, and unusually wide swings in interest rates. At some point Ottawa will have to face up to ways of decoupling Canadian interest rates from extraordinarily high and volatile U.S. rates. In January 1982 several Western countries announced their plan to pursue a more independent interest rate policy from the U.S. Canada, however, does not in 1982 have their advantages of relatively low inflation rates and improving current account balances. Thus, in Canada's case, a decoupling of interest rates could involve the possibility of a further currency devaluation. But the inflationary effect of a devaluation must be judged over a longer period of time rather than in terms of the currency's temporary level. While a more stable interest rate environment in Canada would cause wider fluctuations in the Canadian dollar, this does not mean that the average exchange rate would be much different from what it is under present practices.

Chapter 4 focused on the special problems involved with financing large energy projects. Canadian governments and businesses have always been involved in the financing of megaprojects, but the expected wave of project financing in the future is particularly heavy, and unusually centralized in Alberta. Moreover, there are often overlapping government jurisdictions and regulations which are involved in the approval of these projects. The new wave of projects will be financed against a background of fairly high inflation and record high interest rates, according to the assumptions adopted in this study.

This chapter provides two illustrations of the frustrations and the ingenious financial packaging needed for project financing when government regulation and approval is involved, and argues that government involvement is virtually guaranteed in any case because of the large sums of money and the heavy risks involved — private investors would normally shun these projects unless offered some type of guarantee. The problem with large project financing is that government involvement, although necessary, tends further to deter the attraction of private capital because it sets up a completely new level of risk for the investor. In particular, the risk of delay in an inflationary, high interest rate environment becomes very costly to those making these project financing calculations.

Will the 1980s be an appropriate time in Canada's history to finance this large wave of capital spending? Most long-term studies of the Canadian economy suggest that despite the huge amounts involved in energy financing alone, the domestic savings which will be generated by the economy should be sufficient for financing purposes. But there are some new financing difficulties that surfaced in the 1970s which will continue to be around in the 1980s, in particular, the drying up of the corporate bond market as a place in which to raise large sums of fixed-term money, unusually high real interest rates, and the issue of allocating the investment risk in a regulatory environment.

The projections presented in chapter 1 indicated that the Canadian capital markets will probably be able to generate the requisite volume of savings. The real challenge will be in bringing together the risk capital with the borrower who requires the funds and in establishing suitable terms. Indeed, the basic conclusion of this chapter is that it is not the total size of credit demands in the 1980s which will prove difficult for the capital markets and the economy, but rather the megaproject character of much of the capital investment spending. From the perspective of investors, portfolio diversification alternatives in Canada are very limited, particularly since much of the wave of large project investment in one way or another is tied to the energy sector or to energy prices. All this means that the foreign capital markets will continue to be tapped in the 1980s in a very heavy way because of these portfolio realities. This situation represents a continued public policy dilemma for a federal government committed to reducing the role of foreign investment in Canada.

Chapter 5 explored the ramifications of the Canadianization goal for the financial markets and indirectly for the economy. Canadianization involves the conversion of ownership or control of non-residential equity located within Canada. In order for the Canadianization program actually to be successful, it must involve some repatriation of capital abroad. But the balance of payments impact of an external repatriation of capital is always negative, as witnessed by the heavy outflows of capital during the first six months of 1981. Indeed, the balance of payments impacts from such Canadianization transactions are identical to the effects that can occur through a shift of indigenous Canadian-controlled investment abroad. The crux of this is that Canadianization and/or any induced flight of capital out of Canada will immediately depress the external value of the Canadian currency and may over time have an additional depressing effect, depending upon the true worth of the takeover. In 1981 such a combination of events occurred under adverse balance of payments circumstances. The U.S. central bank was pursuing a policy of extraordinarily high interest rates and the U.S. government had developed an economic climate that was viewed as far more hospitable to business than the climate in Canada. At that time virtually all currencies fell in value with respect to the U.S. dollar, though the actual decline of the Canadian dollar against the U.S. currency was mild in comparison with other currencies — a 5.8 per cent decline measured between August 4, 1981 and its averaged 1980 value. It was also at that time that a takeover and merger wave occurred spontaneously in both Canada and the U.S., and this wave of activity was spurred on by the unusually low prices for petroleum companies caused by a world glut in crude oil. This tended to weaken the Canadian currency even further, as Canadian companies were financing acquisitions in the U.S. through the Canadian banking system. Thus in the short term, the Canadianization objectives of the NEP seemed to depress the Canadian dollar, potentially providing stronger economic growth but also causing higher import inflation.

Moreover, while it seems that a favourable balance of payment position is a necessary condition for a successful Canadianization program, in fact this is not the case. Even with current account deficits, a simple exchange of the kinds of foreign capital inflows into Canada can result in some Canadianization, but this of course does not eliminate Canada's need for foreign capital. Even if the balance of payments were in a surplus position, this need not lead to higher domestic ownership of equity in Canada, as Canadian investors may be attracted to invest in the U.S. or other economies at that time.

For what it is worth, the remaining amount of Canadianization necessary to meet the NEP's objective of 50 per cent Canadian ownership of upstream oil and gas facilities would amount to about $12 billion in 1981 prices. This amount of asset switching is manageable as long as it occurs gradually. But if the currency is weak, careful consideration must be given to the timing considerations so that future runs on the Canadian dollar could be weathered without a policy crisis developing. Indeed it is suggested in this study that an ideal time for a future policy thrust in the direction of Canadianization would be when the Canadian dollar was vastly overvalued and was creating problems for the domestic economy. It is entirely possible that such a scenario could develop some time over the medium term if Canada develops a petro-currency image and, as a result of that image, is swamped by an inflow of capital, which in turn elevates the Canadian currency. As long as the Canadian economy is in such a fundamentally weak balance of payments position, and as long as Canada's inflation rate is in excess of that in the U.S., one certainly should not expect too much spontaneous Canadianization to occur.

Spontaneous Canadianization in other industries will likely not emerge even under the best of the balance of payments scenarios; thus, if further Canadianization objectives are desired, these policies will have to be propelled through the public sector — either federal or provincial — much as has happened under the NEP.

Chapter 6 is concerned with the shift of regional financial power to western Canada, in line with the fact that western economic prospects in the 1980s seem so much stronger than those in the older industrial regions of eastern Canada. There is a mistaken view about that in the context of regional economic growth Canada faces a zero-sum game, that the West's gain is at the expense of eastern Canada. It is pointed out in this chapter that the weak economic performance of eastern Canada in the 1970s was only indirectly related to western economic power. The real culprit in this case was higher international oil prices and the fact that the demand for crude oil is price inelastic. It was the exercise of market power by the OPEC countries which caused the enormous terms of trade shift that has been to the advantage of western Canada. The fact that eastern Canada has suffered because of higher energy prices and the terms of trade shift cannot really be attributed to western Canada, for if the East did not have access to western oil at below world prices, the real income squeeze in the populous eastern provinces would have been even more severe. On the general economic front, there appears to have been very little real economic diversification within the western provinces, despite their improved economic prospects. The notion that eastern Canada is worse off as a result of western prosperity is simply wrong.

But what of the financial market implications of these kinds of shifts? Unfortunately, interregional financial flow data are very sketchy and are simply not available to comment directly on the issue. But it has been noted, for example, that the regional distribution of the directors of the five largest chartered banks has not really changed all that much over the past ten years. Indeed to the extent that there has been some increase in western representation among financial directorships, this seems to reflect more a sudden increase in the size of western-based companies than any basic change in the structure of the financial industry. Thus far the cities of eastern Canada, particularly Toronto and to a lesser extent Montreal, still are, and will likely continue to be, the dominant centres for raising financial capital in Canada. The Alberta government has been setting aside part of its resource-based revenues into the Alberta Heritage Trust and Savings Fund. This fund has grown very rapidly and potentially could be used as a means of attracting investment into western Canada, though so far this has not been done. Thus far one cannot accuse the Alberta government of offering any new kinds of investment incentives that are not offered elsewhere.

More worrisome is the general concern that the provinces will become involved in more direct competition among each other for attracting investment funds. That is, there is a possibility that investment subsidies will become much more a part of the picture in the 1980s than they were in the 1970s, and this is a financial concern to policy makers. All provincial governments seem to be gearing up for much more of this kind of activity, and in this case there almost is a zero-sum game involved.

Finally, while it is true that Canada has a tremendous inventory of investment projects on the drawing board, estimated to amount to about $430 billion of investment spending requirements over the next two decades, still over 50 per cent of that spending will occur outside of western Canada. Even though the West, and Alberta in particular, will reap a disproportionate share of this future wave of investment spending, there are positive spin-offs to Ontario and the rest of the country because of the fact that western Canada likely will not diversify its industries much beyond the limited extent it has already.

Chapter 7 considered the housing market and problems created by generally high interest rates and government policies in Canada. According to most demographic projections, Canada's housing industry should be entering a period of secular slowdown in the 1980s because of the projected decline in new family formation levels. In fact, that secular drop may have began back in 1977, since in 1980 new housing starts fell to the lowest levels since 1966 and the housing slump which began in the mid-1970s had become the longest slump since the 1930s.

While record high mortgage interest rates were the precipitating factor in the slump, government involvement in the housing industry since the mid-1970s has also often proved counterproductive. Rent controls, for example, were imposed in every province under the AIB program in 1976, and are still in force in most provinces. Other federal interventions in the housing industry, which were designed to provide incentives to construct rental units, simply did not quantitatively make much of a dent on this depressed part of the housing market.

Against this background, housing inflation itself, although rather erratic, tended in the 1970s to keep up with the general rate of inflation across the country. Nevertheless, housing inflation has been particularly steep in the major cities of western Canada which experienced a population and business boom, and in Toronto in eastern Canada. It is clear that the social cleavage caused by housing inflation between the "haves" and the "have nots" has increased.

Extremely high mortgage interest rates were shown to have a very uneven incidence across family groups in the country. It was noted that those homeowners faced with costly rollovers at much higher mortgage rates and often with shorter terms, probably, at least, were able to achieve untaxed capital gains in the values of their houses; their problems must therefore be regarded as one of liquidity rather than one of not keeping up with inflation. That is, there are both winners and losers in the high inflation and high mortgage interest rate situation. The winners have seen their assets increase in nominal value, while the losers have seen the cost of financing rise. In many cases the winners and the losers tend to be the same individuals.

However, the incidence of higher mortgage interest rates on the first-house purchaser tends to be very uneven. Statistically it can be shown that families living in cities with high real estate prices, such as Vancouver, Toronto, Calgary and Edmonton, are hurt disproportionately as they tend to be squeezed out of their first house purchase.

The mortgage market, just like all the capital markets, has adjusted rather creatively to the ravages of high inflation. Gradual payment mortgages or shared appreciation mortgages have been introduced into the marketplace, but despite their ingenuity, they cannot erase the high cost of housing finance, particularly the costs facing the first-house buyer. It is clear that interest rate stability, lower real interest rates and lower mortgage rates generally would remove much of the difficulties facing first-time house purchasers in Canada.

Chapter 8 considered the public and private financing of pension funds from a flow-of-funds perspective. This chapter is concerned with such issues as the real rates returned to private pension plans and the mix of assets that will likely be available to them in future years. Through much of the 1970s private pension plans were unable to earn high enough real rates of return because they incurred massive losses on their fixed-interest investments, a situation that has continued into 1982. The chapter also focused on the question of the funding of the Canadian social security plans (particularly the CPP) and the impact of social security savings on national savings and government financing. Two key conclusions are quite obvious with respect to the CPP: it is not going broke, though a higher contribution rate will be required in the future, and it will not be a major source of provincial government finance in the future, as it was in the past.

The chapter accepts the general proposition that during the 1980s the flow of savings into private pension institutions and funds will exceed total gross savings, and that the private pension fund industry will be shifting its assets more in the direction of provincial debt, shorter-term federal government bonds and the equity market, and away from the mortgage market.

Recommendations

A series of glaring economic problems for the Canadian capital markets and the Canadian economy were highlighted in this study. As far as the sources of difficulty for the financial markets are concerned three factors seem to predominate: high inflation, unusually high and volatile interest rates, and the saving and investment distortions that result from the interaction between inflation and the tax system.

146

The recommendations set out below follow from the issues considered in this report:

1. Wage-Price Freeze and Incomes Policy
The federal government should impose a 90-day wage-price freeze to be followed by the introduction of a tax-based incomes policy.

High inflation in Canada continues to be one of the central problems for the economy and the capital markets, and the federal government should not shrink from introducing an incomes policy to supplement and even make more efficient its present anti-inflationary policies. While the subject of incomes policies is somewhat outside of the scope of this study, the case for a Canadian incomes policy (preferably using an anti-inflationary tax-based "incentives" scheme) is even more overwhelming in 1982 than it was several years ago.[1] Depending upon the type of scheme chosen, a tax-based incomes policy (TIP) uses the personal or corporate tax system to coerce (in the penalty case) or induce (with the use of tax incentives) business and labour to comply with lower inflationary wage and price increases. The advantage of the TIP approach is its versatility, its use of the market system to affect anti-inflationary behaviour in contrast with direct controls on wages and prices, and the fact that it would not require a large bureaucracy.

The 90-day wage and price freeze would serve to reduce immediately Canada's inflation rate, would provide an appropriate anti-inflation shock to expectations, and would provide policy makers with some room to manoeuvre in designing an effective tax-based anti-inflation plan. Canada's economic prospects have also been irrationally hurt by fears that the currency will devalue with respect to the U.S. dollar. If an effective TIP policy were in place, it would permit Canada to adopt more stable and lower interest rates, and the need to protect the Canadian dollar using high interest rates would seem less urgent.

2. Interest Rates and Money Supply Objectives
The Bank of Canada should maintain a better balance between interest rates and money supply objectives. The bank should attempt, as quickly as possible, to reduce short-term interest rates.

While interest rate objectives may have carried too much weight in monetary policy considerations prior to 1975, their virtual exclusion since that date as an important policy target is equally wrong. Under present central banking practice interest rates are manipulated either to achieve a desired growth rate in the money supply or to defend the external value of the dollar. Canada's unsatisfactory economic

147

experience since 1975 indicates how harmful such practices have been for the economy. A more balanced monetary policy is required, and that balance must recognize the importance of both interest rates and money supply growth rates. There is no need to abandon Canada's longer-term money supply growth objectives, but this strategy must be approached with far less rigidity than has been practised in recent years.

The unusual harshness of the current monetary policy, with its associated high real interest rates and unusually variable interest rates, is imposing an excessive burden on the Canadian economy in terms of lost jobs and output and in terms of high numbers of business failures. Inflation in 1982 has barely yielded to the harsh levels of economic restraint that are in place. If excess spending were the chief source of Canada's inflation problem, then the economy's inflation rate would have responded far better to the levels of economic restraint than it has thus far. The Bank of Canada can still pursue its anti-inflation monetary policy with substantially lower interest rates, that is with interest rates several percentage points in excess of the rate of inflation.

3. The Tax System
The federal government should review the Canadian tax system from the perspective of eliminating some of the glaring saving and investment distortions resulting from high inflation.

Inflation results in an overstatement of corporate income and increases the effective tax rate unevenly among companies. An increase in the rate of inflation also automatically increases the personal tax rate of individuals receiving fixed interest earnings. One cannot condone the serious distortion of savings and investment decisions, nor the actual reduction in private capital investment, which results from a tax system that does not fully acknowledge that inflation exists.

At a minimum, the federal government should consider increasing the tax-free allowance for interest and dividend income from the present $1,000 level for individuals. Similarly, the corporate tax system should be overhauled so as to reduce the uneven burden which inflation imposes on firms, and to reduce the general overstatement of corporate income which results from inflation.

4. Long-Term Investment
The federal government should develop a set of policies to encourage long-term investment.

148

A major problem at this time is the lack of long-term investment in Canada. Even if interest rates decline substantially from their high 1982 levels, the liquidity position of the Canadian economy could still remain unbalanced for some time.

Two manifestations of this problem are the inability of corporations to issue long-term debt at affordable interest rates and the related difficulty of financing long-term corporate bonds and household mortgages. While it is difficult to see how long-term investment can be encouraged in a high interest rate environment, some remedial fiscal measures might be helpful.

Because of these funding difficulties, Ottawa should consider providing some tax incentives to corporations (and to savers) which would result in a stretching out of the average term of debt. This could take the form of a tax incentive scheme such as the taxing of interest earnings from longer-term investments at a lower rate than earnings derived from short-term investments.

5. The Financing of Megaprojects
Governments should consider introducing measures to reduce the costs of financing future megaprojects.

Despite the recent setbacks with respect to the economic viability of many large-scale investment projects in western Canada, there seems little question that at some time in the future many of these projects will become reactivated. At that future time many of the same problems will be in place, particularly the risks associated with investing in large projects which offer returns so far in the future, as well as the investor risk related to government regulations. Indeed, governments should try to smooth out as much as feasible the regulatory process which delays the start-up and completion of projects.

To the extent that the regulatory process raises the total cost of these projects, there might be some advantage if governments provided completion guarantees or borrowing cost guarantees simply to get some of these projects off the ground. Government guarantees would also make it possible to finance large-scale projects more easily in the Canadian capital markets than in foreign markets. If public funds are involved in this way (via government guarantees) and if the public is to share directly in the risks of these projects, then the public should also share in the potential upside revenue gains stemming out of these investments.

6. The Canadianization Program

Future Canadianization measures must be considered in the context of Canada's fragile balance of payments position. The Bank of Canada should be involved at an early stage in such cases so as to smooth out any adverse balance of payments effects.

The exchange rate crisis of 1981 was due to many factors, and to the extent that the Canadianization program added additional pressures, some pre-planning with respect to the balance of payments would have helped. The lesson that emerged out of the exchange rate crisis is that when the economy is unusually weak, a sudden rush of capital out of Canada can create a major short-term policy problem for the government. These problems can be minimized if not fully avoided.

As much as possible, future public sector initiatives in the direction of furthering Canadianizing of industry should be timed so as to minimize any possible disruptive effect on the Canadian balance of payments and on the Canadian dollar. Ideally such policies should be promoted when the current account is strengthening and moving towards a surplus. More cooperation is required among the Department of Finance, the Bank of Canada, and other related departments (in the 1981 case it was the Department of Energy, Mines and Resources) to ensure that the balance of payments effects will be managed more smoothly. Future initiatives in this direction should involve the Bank of Canada as early as possible so that it can take steps to minimize the exchange rate difficulties.

7. The Housing Industry

As a temporary measure, Ottawa should provide some mortgage interest rate relief to those rolling over or taking out new residential mortgages.

Canada's housing industry is in its longest slump since the Great Depression. If mortgage interest rates fell substantially, the housing slump would end. Failing this, some temporary fiscal relief should also be provided to the homeowner. While there are many possible avenues for temporarily subsidizing mortgage interest costs, two alternative methods seem appropriate. Ottawa could permit the deduction of a shelter cost allowance which would apply to all individuals, including those experiencing high rental cost increases. Alternatively, Ottawa could introduce a type of "marginal" mortgage interest rate deductibility scheme, but with a cap to limit the amount of the maximum deduction and with a sunset clause during which it would be hoped that nominal and real interest rates would come down.

150

The marginal mortgage interest rate deductibility plan would become effective, for example, on interest payments in excess of 13 per cent. Thus if the average mortgage rate was 19 per cent in 1982, the tax payer would be able to deduct 6/19 or 31.6 per cent of his calendar year mortgage payments. Either scheme, the shelter cost allowance or the marginal mortgage deductible scheme should operate as a refundable tax credit to ensure that those individuals who pay no taxes also obtain the tax benefits.

Three separate recommendations originally put forward by this writer and Douglas D. Peters in *The Monetarist Counter-Revolution*[2] bear repeating.

8. A Medium-Term Policy for the Balance of Payments

The Canadian authorities should boldy accept the medium-term policy objective of attempting to balance Canada's current account in goods and services. If Canada achieved this objective it would be consistent with no net losses or gains of jobs and output to the rest of the world over the medium term.

9. Policies to Develop the Canadian Capital Markets

Ottawa should reinstate the guidelines in force from 1970 to 1974 that Canadian borrowers search out domestic sources of funds before considering long-term foreign issues. Moreover, it is argued that if external financing is deemed appropriate for the economy, the federal government rather than the provinces or other borrowers should be the principal issuer of securities in the foreign markets. Finally, the Canadian government should also encourage the necessary institutional changes to increase access to loanable funds within Canada. Among such changes, the Bank of Canada should include in its list of eligible assets for secondary reserves marketable provincial securities and provincial treasury bills. This change would in no way change the efficiency of monetary policy, but it might permit improved access to restricted pools of funds for other borrowing groups.

10. The Disclosure of Monetary Policy Formulation

The process of monetary policy formulation in Canada should be opened up more to the public than it is at present. The more open disclosure practices of the U.S. Federal Reserve System should become a model for a Canadian plan. A similar framework could be developed for Canada which could be consistent with Canada's political system and central banking structure.

Appendix

A Postscript on the Balance of Payments Constraint on Economic Policy Making in Canada

Canada, unlike the U.S., is a net international debtor. As the figures in Table A-1 illustrate, Canada's total net indebtedness rose to about $69.5 billion in 1980 on a book value basis. On the liability side of the ledger, Canada's total international liabilities amounted to about $135.5 billion in 1979, rather equally distributed between liabilities due to foreign direct investment and to foreign portfolio investment. On the asset side of that ledger, direct investments abroad by Canadians amounted to about $19 billion in 1979 and $23.5 billion in 1980.

Canada's international indebtedness has risen swiftly in nominal terms, primarily because of Canada's borrowing of debt capital abroad and because of the attraction of equity investment into this country. But in fact the increase in foreign direct investment in Canada in recent years has been primarily due to foreign-controlled firms operating in Canada, essentially reinvesting their retained earnings generated by their Canadian operations.

The swift increase in Canada's overall international indebtedness during the second half of the 1970s had its direct counterpart in the worsening current accounts statistics. As the statistics in Table A-2 show, since 1974, with one exception, Canada's current account deficit exceeded $3.5 billion, although in 1980 an unexpectedly favourable merchandise trade improvement occurred and the current account deficit declined to $1.5 billion. While it is widely recognized that the source of the current account problem is centred in the service payment outflows (the net outflows amounted to $10 billion in 1980), few recognize that interest payments outflows are growing much more rapidly than dividend outflows.

TABLE A-1
THE CANADIAN BALANCE OF INTERNATIONAL INDEBTEDNESS, 1951-80
($ billions)

End of Period	Canadian Liabilities				Canadian Assets						Net Cdn Int'l Indebtedness
	Basic Value of Foreign Direct Inv. in Canada[1]	Foreign Portfolio Inv. in Canada	Other Cdn Liabilities to Foreigners	Total	Direct Inv.	Portfolio Inv.	Govt Loans and Subscription	Cdn Net Official Monetary Assets	Other Cdn External Assets	Total	
1951	4.5	5.0	1.8	11.3	1.2	0.5	2.0	1.9	0.3	6.0	5.3
1952	5.2	5.2	1.3	11.7	1.3	0.7	2.0	1.9	0.6	6.4	5.3
1953	6.0	5.4	1.3	12.7	1.5	0.8	1.9	1.9	0.6	6.6	6.1
1954	6.8	5.8	1.4	14.0	1.6	0.8	1.8	2.0	0.8	6.9	7.0
1955	7.7	5.8	1.7	15.2	1.7	0.9	1.7	2.0	0.8	7.1	8.0
1956	8.9	6.8	1.8	17.5	1.9	1.0	1.7	2.0	1.0	7.5	10.1
1957	10.1	7.3	2.2	19.6	2.1	1.0	1.7	1.9	1.3	7.9	11.8
1958	10.9	8.1	2.5	21.5	2.1	1.0	1.6	2.0	1.5	8.5	13.3
1959	11.9	9.0	2.9	23.8	2.3	1.2	1.6	1.9	1.5	8.9	15.3
1960	12.9	9.3	3.4	25.6	2.5	1.3	1.6	2.0	1.5	9.0	16.6
1961	13.7	9.9	3.7	27.3	2.6	1.5	1.5	2.4	1.6	9.6	17.7
1962	14.7	10.2	3.9	28.8	2.8	1.8	1.4	2.6	1.5	10.1	18.7
1963	15.5	10.7	4.3	30.5	3.1	2.0	1.4	2.8	1.6	10.9	19.6
1964	16.0	11.5	5.3	32.8	3.3	2.2	1.6	3.1	2.2	12.4	20.4
1965	17.4	12.3	5.6	35.3	3.5	2.5	1.6	3.3	2.0	12.9	22.4

Canadian Liabilities (columns: Basic Value of Foreign Direct Inv. in Canada[1]; Foreign Portfolio Inv. in Canada; Other Cdn Liabilities to Foreigners; Total) — _Canadian Assets_ (columns: Direct Inv.; Portfolio Inv.; Govt Loans and Subscription; Cdn Net Official Monetary Assets; Other Cdn External Assets; Total) — Net Cdn Int'l Indebtedness

End of Period	Basic Value of Foreign Direct Inv. in Canada[1]	Foreign Portfolio Inv. in Canada	Other Cdn Liabilities to Foreigners	Total	Direct Inv.	Portfolio Inv.	Govt Loans and Subscription	Cdn Net Official Monetary Assets	Other Cdn External Assets	Total	Net Cdn Int'l Indebtedness
1966	19.0	13.2	5.7	37.9	3.7	3.0	1.6	2.9	2.7	13.9	24.0
1967	20.7	14.0	5.8	40.5	4.0	3.4	1.6	2.9	3.3	15.2	25.3
1968	22.5	15.5	6.3	44.3	4.6	3.7	1.6	3.3	4.8	18.0	26.3
1969	24.4	17.3	6.9	48.6	5.2	3.8	1.6	3.3	6.6	20.5	28.1
1970	26.4	17.8	7.8	52.0	6.2	3.8	1.8	4.7	7.1	23.6	28.4
1971	28.0	18.5	8.6	55.1	6.5	4.4	1.9	5.6	8.0	26.4	28.7
1972	29.7	20.6	8.7	59.0	6.7	5.1	2.1	6.0	9.3	29.2	29.8
1973	32.9	22.2	9.8	64.9	7.8	5.9	2.3	5.8	11.3	33.1	31.8
1974	36.4	24.2	12.3	72.9	9.2	7.0	2.6	5.8	13.0	37.6	35.3
1975	37.4	29.0	14.3	83.4	10.5	8.0	3.0	5.4	14.1	41.0	42.4
1976	40.3	38.4	16.0	94.7	11.5	8.6	3.4	5.9	19.4	48.8	45.9
1977	43.7	44.0	18.1	109.1	13.5	10.1	3.9	5.1	22.6	55.1	54.0
1978	48.2	49.3[2]	19.5[2]	119.3[2]	16.3[2]	11.1	4.5[2]	2.2	24.3	58.0	61.3[2]
1979	51.0	54.6[2]	26.3[2]	135.5[2]	19.0[2]	12.8[2]	4.7[2]	4.2	24.8[2]	66.0[2]	69.5[2]
1980	54.5	54.6[2]	26.3[2]		23.5[2]						

Notes: [1] End of period.
[2] Estimate.

Source: Statistics Canada, _Canada's International Investment Position_ (Cat. No. 67-202)/January 1981 and _Bank of Canada Review_, February 1981.

TABLE A-2
THE BALANCE OF PAYMENTS ON CURRENT ACCOUNT, MERCHANDISE TRADE, SERVICES AND TRANSFERS, 1946-80
($ millions)

Year	Merchandise Trade			Services	Transfers	Current Account Balance
	Exports	Imports	Balance			
1946	2,393	1,822	571	−151	−57	363
1947	2,723	2,535	188	−118	−21	49
1948	3,030	2,598	432	−7	26	451
1949	2,989	2,696	293	−142	26	177
1950	3,139	3,132	7	−341	15	−319
1951	3,950	4,101	−151	−377	16	−512
1952	4,339	3,854	485	−299	1	187
1953	4,152	4,212	−60	−378	−10	−448
1954	3,934	3,916	18	−436	−6	−424
1955	4,332	4,543	−211	−442	−34	−687
1956	4,837	5,565	−728	−599	−45	−1,372
1957	4,894	5,488	−594	−806	−51	−1,451
1958	4,890	5,066	−176	−836	−125	−1,137
1959	5,151	5,572	−421	−953	−113	−1,487
1960	5,392	5,540	−148	−959	−126	−1,233
1961	5,889	5,716	173	−1,029	−72	−928
1962	6,387	6,203	184	−995	−19	−830
1963	7,082	6,579	503	−996	−28	−521
1964	8,238	7,537	701	−1,111	−14	−424
1965	8,745	8,627	118	−1,277	29	−1,130
1966	10,326	10,102	224	−1,438	52	−1,162
1967	11,338	10,772	566	−1,137	72	−449
1968	13,720	12,249	1,471	−1,752	184	−97
1969	15,035	14,071	964	−2,024	143	−917
1970	16,921	13,869	3,052	−2,099	153	1,106
1971	17,877	15,314	2,563	−2,398	266	431
1972	20,129	18,272	1,857	−2,527	284	−386
1973	25,461	22,726	2,735	−2,971	344	108
1974	32,591	30,902	1,689	−3,706	557	−1,460
1975	33,511	33,962	−451	−4,686	380	−4,757
1976	37,995	36,607	1,388	−5,760	530	−3,842
1977	44,253	41,523	2,730	−7,444	413	−4,301
1978	52,752	49,151	3,601	−8,690	43	−5,046
1979	65,170	61,198	3,972	−9,732	662	−5,098
1980	76,106	68,153	7,953	−10,737	1,246	−1,538

Source: *Bank of Canada Review*, various issues.

Most of the portfolio investment in Canada generates interest outflows, rather than dividend outflows. In any event, the data in Table A-3 indicate that during the postwar period the annual net dividend outflows exceeded the outflows for interest payments until 1972, when the situation sharply reversed. In 1980, for example, net interest outflows amounted to $3.9 billion, while net dividend outflows amount to $1.6 billion.

On the capital account side of the balance of payments ledger, the propensity for Canadian governments and institutions to issue long-term bonds in foreign countries, primarily the U.S., is very marked. The data presented in Table A-4 show that since 1974 the annual value of new bond issues has ranged between a high flow of $7 billion to a low flow of about $2.5 billion.

The important public policy issue here is that the current account is usually in deficit because of fairly substantial interest and dividend payments abroad, while on the capital accounts side, Canadian institutions rely quite heavily on U.S. financial institutions and markets for their long-term financing requirements. Foreign direct investment in Canada continues to grow, although this stems primarily from the reinvested earnings of the branch operations in this country. It is interesting to note that even in the early 1970s when Canada recorded current account surpluses on its balance of payments, this country still remained a net borrower of long-term funds and a net lender of short-term funds to the U.S. In the early 1980s Canada remains a net borrower of both long-term and short-term funds, as both sources of funds are used to finance the current account deficit.

Back in 1970 when Canada was a net exporter of short-term capital and a net importer of long-term capital, Andrew Brimmer, then with the Federal Reserve System, argued that the Canadian capital markets were structurally deficient. At that time Brimmer was expressing an official U.S. concern that Canada was too reliant on the U.S. long-term bond market. Brimmer argued that it was in the U.S. interest, as well as Canada's, for Canada to switch some of its long-term borrowing back into the Canadian marketplace. The crux of the Brimmer argument was that imperfections in the Canadian capital markets helped explain why Canadian borrowers tended to resort very heavily to the long-term debt markets in the U.S. If one accepted the Brimmer proposition, one could extend it to imply that some form of restructuring of the Canadian capital markets was necessary in order to lower Canada's reliance on international capital to balance its current account deficit.

Neufeld[1] disagreed with the Brimmer argument, as Neufeld did not

TABLE A-3
THE BALANCE OF PAYMENTS ON NON-MERCHANDISE ACCOUNT, 1951-80
($ millions)

Year	Gold Production Available for Export	Travel (Net)	Interest (Net)	Dividends (Net)	Freight and Shipping (Net)	Other Services	Withholding Tax	Total Services	Transfers	Total Services and Transfers	Net Undistributed Earnings on Foreign Direct Investment in Canada
1951	150	−6	−60	−277	−3	−125	−56	−377	16	−361	—
1952	150	−66	−54	−207	8	−75	−55	−299	1	−298	—
1953	144	−63	−58	−184	−56	−107	−54	−378	−10	−388	305
1954	155	−84	−77	−200	−43	−129	−58	−436	−6	−442	260
1955	155	−121	−73	−239	−17	−80	−67	−442	−34	−476	335
1956	147	−161	−90	−292	−45	−89	−69	−599	−45	−644	400
1957	144	−162	−110	−331	−70	−194	−83	−806	−51	−857	425
1958	157	−193	−118	−329	−59	−246	−48	−836	−125	−961	235
1959	148	−207	−140	−351	−105	−224	−74	−953	−113	−1,066	350
1960	162	−207	−163	−322	−91	−259	−79	−959	−126	−1,085	280
1961	162	−160	−180	−371	−82	−282	−116	−1,029	−72	−1,101	240
1962	155	−43	−194	−387	−86	−315	−125	−995	−19	−1,014	325
1963	154	24	−215	−415	−85	−332	−127	−996	−28	−1,024	435
1964	145	−50	−251	−427	−35	−353	−140	−1,111	−14	−1,125	480
1965	138	−49	−289	−475	−93	−342	−167	−1,277	29	−1,248	735
1966	127	−60	−319	−503	−65	−414	−204	−1,438	52	−1,386	640
1967	112	−423	−369	−547	−31	−507	−218	−1,137	72	−1,065	845
1968	33	−29	−444	−462	−40	−601	−209	−1,752	184	−1,568	810
1969	—	−214	−489	−426	−61	−600	−234	−2,024	143	−1,881	1,045
1970	—	−216	−503	−519	20	−612	−269	−2,099	153	−1,946	830

Year	Gold Production Available for Export	Travel (Net)	Interest (Net)	Dividends (Net)	Freight and Shipping (Net)	Other Services	With-holding Tax	Total Services	Transfers	Total Services and Transfers	Net Undistributed Earnings on Foreign Direct Investment in Canada
1971	—	−202	−535	−606	−12	−765	−278	−2,398	266	−2,132	1,335
1972	—	−234	−605	−443	−74	−884	−287	−2,527	284	−2,243	1,545
1973	—	−296	−679	−581	−66	−1,027	−322	−2,971	344	−2,627	2,165
1974	—	−284	−686	−867	−224	−1,215	−430	−3,706	557	−3,149	2,730
1975	—	−727	−974	−979	−433	−1,108	−465	−4,686	380	−4,306	2,520
1976	—	−1,191	−1,566	−932	−150	−1,417	−504	−5,760	530	−5,230	2,685
1977	—	−1,641	−2,457	−1,201	−26	−1,585	−534	−7,444	413	−7,031	3,345
1978	—	−1,706	−3,158	−1,341	130	−2,033	−582	−8,690	43	−8,647	3,500[1]
1979	—	−1,068	−3,685	−1,614	290	−2,901	−754	−9,732	662	−9,070	3,500[1]
1980	—	−1,138	−3,946	−1,615	433	−3,476	−995	−10,737	1,246	−9,491	4,100[1]

Note: [1]Estimate arrived at by subtracting flow of direct investment in Canada from book value of foreign direct investment in Canada.

Source: *Bank of Canada Review*, various issues.

TABLE A-4
THE BALANCE OF PAYMENTS ON CAPITAL ACCOUNT, 1974-80
($ millions)

	1974	1975	1976	1977	1978	1979	1980
Capital Movements in Long-Term Form							
Direct investment							
In Canada	845	725	−300	475	85	675	535
Abroad	−810	−915	−590	−740	−2,010	−1,945	−2,675
Transactions in Canadian Stocks	−139	87	−52	−105	−269	513	−1,464
Transactions in Canadian bonds							
Gross new issues	2,409	4,952	8,948	5,876	6,395	5,112	4,897
Retirements	−585	−847	−880	−899	−1,217	−1,923	−1,954
Trade in outstanding bonds	41	302	559	243	35	476	1,071
Transactions in foreign securities	46	−17	79	221	25	−556	−129
Government of Canada loans and subscriptions—advances and repayments	−311	−339	−417	−504	−247	−521	−481
Export credits	−573	−355	−174	−547	−808	−780	−1,106
Other long-term capital movements	118	342	750	245	1,373	1,787	−248
Total long-term capital movements	1,041	3,935	7,923	4,265	3,362	2,838	1,374
Capital Movements in Short-Term Form							
Resident holdings of foreign currencies							
Chartered bank net foreign currency position with non-residents	−1,354	489	−941	1,384	2,771	4,105	1,406
Non-bank holdings of foreign currencies abroad	1,590	−217	−346	−656	−566	136	−528

Non-resident holdings of Canadian assets							
Canadian dollar deposits	597	561	160	230	37	524	-63
Government of Canada demand liabilities	45	-4	7	172	55	217	171
Treasury bills	77	37	440	242	-53	-183	525
Commercial paper	-58	182	514	178	-46	604	698
Finance company paper	138	168	20	42	128	-15	-193
Other finance company obligations	158	-89	47	-55	-15	70	70
Other short-term capital movements n.i.e.	117	493	-887	-1,159	-25	2,483	-910
Total short-term capital movements	1,310	1,620	99	650	1,152	7,846	1,176
Total long- and short-term movements	2,351	5,555	8,022	4,915	4,514	10,684	2,550
Current account balance	-1,460	-4,757	-3,842	-4,301	-5,046	-5,098	-1,538
Net errors and omissions	-867	-1,203	-3,658	-2,035	-2,767	-3,897	-2,510
Allocation of SDRs	—	—	—	—	—	219	217
Net official monetary movements	24	-405	522	-1,421	-3,299	1,908	-1,281

Source: *Bank of Canada Review*, various issues.

regard it as a sign of inefficiently operating markets that Canada relies heavily on capital flows from the U.S. He specifically disagreed with the argument that it was largely because of the existing inefficiencies in the Canadian capital markets that the pattern of the flow of funds into and out of Canada had developed.

In fact, the efficiency-inefficiency debate is completely beside the point. In the narrowest sense, there is no doubt that borrowing long-term capital in the U.S. market is an efficient and natural response in that it broadens the effective size of the marketplace and increases the number of potential suppliers of funds. But the plain facts are that, in the process, Canada's access to the U.S. market contributed to its net international indebtedness, and it is argued here that this debtor status is somewhat self-perpetuating.

In particular, the U.S. exchange rate value of the Canadian dollar — a subjective government priority — has never truly been "freely" determined in the marketplace in the sense that even if the government of the day abrogated direct intervention in determining its U.S. value, it still intervenes indirectly through its interest rate policies which affect the exchange rate. In 1981 Ottawa, in fact, used direct intervention, indirect intervention and moral suasion to defend the dollar.

For example, in mid-1981 the federal finance minister applied moral suasion to the five largest Canadian banks to deter the flow of Canadian-sourced acquisition financing for takeovers in the U.S., which had occurred at a time when the Canadian dollar had plunged to an all-time low of about 80 cents U.S. The other option that could have been pursued at that time was simply to accept the high levels of capital flowing out of Canada and simply to allow the Canadian dollar to depreciate even further.

The federal government obviously believed that the efficiency criteria, which call for non-intervention in the capital markets, would have resulted in an economic management crisis or an exchange crisis. Support for the currency primarily based on higher short-term interest rates was controversial, for there were other options available, such as allowing the currency to depreciate or to have the government intervene more heavily in the foreign exchange market.

The key point here is that macroeconomic management in Canada is made much more difficult because of this country's overall international indebtedness. Policies should be considered which would lessen the indebtedness, for otherwise the Bank of Canada will continue to have very little effective influence on interest rate and exchange rate developments in Canada.

Notes

Chapter 1

[1] Leonard Waverman and Arthur Donner (with Diane Groome), "Investments in Energy Supply Industries and the Economy of the OECD" (Paper prepared for the OECD/IEA, Toronto, May 1981).

[2] This adjustment carries with it a rather poor prognostication for productivity and inflation, since investment is shifting from industries which traditionally have generated rapid productivity growth (such as manufacturing) to the energy sector which generates relatively low productivity growth.

[3] See Royal Trust, "Through A Glass, Darkly: A Medium-Term Canadian Perspective 1981-1986" (November 1981). The author is grateful to Mr. John McTear and Ms. Anna Guthrie for allowing him to utilize the capital market projections provided in the report. The author was also a contributor to the report, though he was not involved in the specific capital market forecast.

Chapter 2

[1] See John Bossons, "The Effect of Inflation-Induced Hidden Wealth Taxes" (Paper presented to the Canadian Tax Foundation conference, Montreal, November 24, 1981), pp. 32-38.

Chapter 3

[1] See Arthur W. Donner and Douglas D. Peters, *The Monetarist Counter-Revolution: A Critique of Canadian Monetary Policy 1975-1979* (Toronto: James Lorimer, 1979).

[2] Gerald K. Bouey, Remarks to the Empire Club of Canada, Toronto, November 13, 1980, in *Bank of Canada Review*, November 1980, p. 8.

[3] Thomas Courchene, however, is dissatisfied with the pace of monetary gradualism in Canada, since the growth rate in the broadly defined monetary aggregates has not slowed down as much as in the narrowly defined case. As well, Courchene is uneasy with the bank's foreign exchange intervention policy. See Thomas J. Courchene, *An Analysis of Monetary Gradualism, 1975-80: Money, Inflation, and the Bank of Canada*, vol. 2 (Montreal: C.D. Howe Research Institute, December 1981).

[4] The real interest rate is a rough measure of true borrowing costs or real returns on invested capital. The real interest rate is also a measure of how restrictive monetary policy actually is. This concept is discussed at greater length later in this chapter.

[5] See the U.S. inflation projection set out in Table 3-1. Since those projections were made, the expected trend rate of U.S. inflation has been considerably revised downwards. Lower U.S. wage settlements, easing OPEC prices, and the 1981-82 international slump played a considerable role in the downward revision of inflationary expectations.

[6] Department of Finance, "The Current Economic Situation and Prospects for the Canadian Economy in the Short and Medium Term" (November 1981), p. 19.

[7] In its base case projection the council forecasts continued high increases in the CPI, ranging from 12.2 per cent in 1982 to a low of 8 per cent in 1989. In contrast to the policies that prevailed between 1976 and 1981, the council argues that "Canadian economic policy must focus on simultaneously reducing inflation and restoring real income growth." See Economic Council of Canada, *Room for Manoeuvre*, Eighteenth Annual Review, 1981, pp. 36, 79.

[8] Ibid., pp. 82, 83.

[9] Ironically, there was a significant shift in the composition of aggregate demand towards investment spending between 1979 and 1981, but this seems to have had little effect on arresting Canada's high rate of inflation.

[10] In 1981 consumer prices rose 12.5 per cent in Canada and 8.9 per cent in the U.S.

[11] John Cornwall, "Do We Need Separate Theories of Inflation and Unemployment?" *Canadian Public Policy*, April 1981, pp. 165-78.

[12] See Donner and Peters, *The Monetarist Counter-Revolution*, pp. 46-50.

Chapter 4

[1] See Department of Energy, Mines and Resources, *An Energy Strategy for Canada* (Ottawa: Information Canada, 1977); Department of Economic Research, Toronto-Dominion Bank, *Business and Economics*, vol. 8, no. 1 (March 1979); and Table 1-4.

[2] John Grant, "The National Energy Program and Canadian Financial Markets," in G. C. Watkins and M. A. Walker, *Reaction: The National Energy Program* (Vancouver: The Fraser Institute, 1981), p. 132.

[3] R. L. Golden and R. M. Freeman, "Raising Long-Term Debt for Project Financing" (Speech given in Toronto, July 29, 1975), p. 3.

[4] Myron J. Gordon, "The Costs and Benefits of Foreign Ownership of a Tar-Sands Plant" (Unpublished paper, January 16, 1981), p. 3.

[5] U.S. Department of the Interior, "Alaskan Natural Gas Transportation Systems: A Report to the Congress Pursuant to Public Law 93-153" (December 1975), p. 149.

[6] Ibid., p. 150.

[7] Golden and Freeman, "Raising Long-Term Debt for Project Financing," p. 12.

[8] "Financing an Alaska Natural Gas Transportation System" (Report to the President by six participating agencies, July 1, 1977), chapter 4, p. 32.

[9] U.S. Department of the Interior, "Alaskan Natural Gas Transportation Systems," p. 167.

[10] Arlon R. Tussing and Connie C. Barlow, *Financing the Alaska Highway Gas Pipeline: What Is To Be Done?* (Institute of Social and Economic Research, University of Alaska, April 1979), p. 1.

Chapter 5

[1] For example, arguments favouring the NEP have been made on grounds that extended beyond the simple objective of national energy self-sufficiency.

[2] Bank of Montreal, "Canada Corporate Takeovers: Some Economic Impacts" (July 28, 1981).

[3] Ibid., p. 12.

[4] Energy, Mines and Resources Canada, *Canada Petroleum Industry Monitoring Survey*, First Six Months 1981, p. 3.

[5] Bank of Montreal, "Canadian Corporate Takeovers," pp. 39-45.

[6] *Canadian Petroleum Industry Monitoring Survey*, 1979, p. 26.

[7] See *Canadian Petroleum Industry Monitoring Survey*, First Six Months 1981.

[8] Graham N. Notman, an oil and gas analyst with Research Securities of Canada Ltd., suggested in 1982 that the ratio of market to book valuation for most major petroleum companies in Canada was about 2.5 to 1.

[9] Statistics Canada, *Corporations and Labour Unions Return Act Report for 1977 — Part I, Corporations*, January 1981, p. 9.

[10] Ibid., p. 97.

[11] H. L. Robinson, "Notes on Financing Canadianization" (Paper given at a conference sponsored by the Committee for the Canadianization of the Petroleum Industry, Ottawa, January 23, 1981), p. 2.

[12] In 1981 major sums of Canadian monies moved into the U.S. real estate and energy industries. Canadian-based oil companies shifted some of their investment in response to a more hospitable government climate and higher perceived returns in the U.S., as well as in protest against Canada's NEP.

Chapter 6

[1] For example, one often hears the concern that a massive withdrawal of OPEC and other foreign-held U.S. dollar assets from the U.S. banks could trigger an international financial collapse and a run on the U.S. dollar. Indeed, a large scale depreciation of the U.S. dollar could occur if OPEC simply attempted to diversify its foreign assets holdings at the expense of U.S. assets. But aside from the international disaster scenario, there is a concern over the vast growth of the unregulated Eurodollar market and the supposed mismatch between OPEC short-term deposits and the longer-term commitments that Western banks have extended based on these deposits. The Canadian parallel to these concerns is very remote, and the existence of a national banking system ensures this to be the case.

[2] Richard Simeon, "Natural Resource Revenues and Canadian Federalism: A Survey of the Issues," *Canadian Public Policy* VI, Supplement (February 1980), p. 183.

[3] See Department of Finance, *Economic Review*, April 1981, pp. 126, 127.

[4] A. D. Scott, "The Causes of Regional Disparity," in N. H. Lithwick, *Regional Economic Policy: The Canadian Experience* (Toronto: McGraw-Hill Ryerson, 1978), p. 50.

[5] Kenneth H. Norrie and Michael B. Percy, "Westward Shift and Interregional Adjustment: A Preliminary Assessment," Economic Council of Canada Discussion Paper No. 201 (May 1981).

[6] See Tom Sindlinger, "The Heritage Fund," draft study (1981).

[7] Andrew G. Kniewasser, "The Effect of the AHSTF on Capital Markets," *Canadian Public Policy* VI, Supplement (February 1980), p. 245.

[8] Ibid., p. 246.

[9] Thomas J. Courchene and James R. Melvin, "Energy Revenues: Consequences for the Rest of Canada," *Canadian Public Policy* VI, Supplement (February 1980), p. 203.

[10] Norrie and Percy, "Westward Shift and Interregional Adjustment," pp. 109, 111.

[11] Ibid., Table IV-II.

[12] David Perry et al., "A Round-Up of Provincial Budgets," *Canadian Tax Journal*, vol. 27, no. 41 (July-August 1979), p. 457.

[13] Judith Maxwell and Caroline Pestieau, *Economic Realities of Contemporary Confederation* (Montreal: C. D. Howe Research Institute, 1980), chapters 6 and 7.

[14] Norrie and Percy, "Westward Shift and Interregional Adjustment," p. 132.

Chapter 7

[1] Canada Mortgage and Housing Corporation, *Housing Requirements Model: Projections to 2000* (Ottawa: CMHC, March 1978), p. 21.

[2] The shortening of the maturity of mortgages in itself creates more uncertainty for borrowers but is of course a natural response from the lender's perspective.

[3] See E. Wayne Clendenning, *The Viability of Rental Construction, the Effect of Rent Control, and Strategies for a Smooth Return to a Fully Viable Rental Sector* (Ottawa: CMHC, November 1980).

[4] Canada Mortgage and Housing Corporation, *Canadian Housing Statistics 1979* (Ottawa: CMHC, March 1980), Table 9.

[5] This statistic was provided by a CMHC official.

[6] Department of Finance, "Government of Canada Tax Expenditure Account," December 1980, p. 22.

[7] Canada Mortgage and Housing Corporation, *Quarterly Housing Outlook and Economic Forecast*, February 1981, p. 3.

[8] Canada Mortgage and Housing Corporation, *Special Report: Effect of Interest Rate Changes on Affordability of Housing by Market User* (Ottawa: CMHC, 1980).

Chapter 8

[1] Task Force on Retirement Income Policy, *The Retirement Income System in Canada: Problems and Alternative Policies for Reform*, vols. I and II (Ottawa: Canadian Government Publishing Centre, 1979), and Economic Council of Canada, *One In Three: Pensions for Canadians to 2030* (Ottawa: Canadian Government Publishing Centre, 1979). The Ontario Royal Commission (1981) made two important recommendations to the Ontario government which are relevant to the issues raised in this chapter. First, the Royal Commission recommended that a system of mandatory private pension plans (PURS) be established under which all employers could make contributions and all employees would participate. Secondly, the commission recommended that pensioners' benefits should be indexed through the use of an inflation tax credit. See William M. Mercer Ltd., *The Mercer Bulletin*, November 1981.

[2] Employers and employees each contribute 1.8 per cent of the employee's earnings, for an aggregate contribution of 3.6 per cent of the earnings base. The earnings base is calculated as the difference between the year's maximum pensionable earnings (the YMPE) and the year's basic exemption (YBE). Altogether in 1977, CPP, QPP and OAS benefit payments represented about 3.5 per cent of total personal income in Canada, and the contributions into the scheme amounted to 22.7 per cent of personal direct taxes and just over 4 per cent of total personal income. For 1977, average monthly benefits paid under the CPP/QPP reached $173.61, 15.9 per cent of average wages and salaries.

166

[3] See *The Mercer Bulletin*, March 1970.

Canadian pension law, based on provincial legislation, has fairly common vesting features across the country. For instance, it requires vesting to take place after the employee has passed his forty-fifth birthday and has ten years of service. Some plans provide more liberal arrangements for vesting — for example, some require only ten years of service with no limitation on age, while some even allow less than ten years of service before vesting occurs. The federal civil service plans are the most generous in this respect, since they provide more favourable vesting arrangements than are found in the private sector.

[4] Various issues of *The Mercer Bulletin* have followed the development of the pension debate very closely. See the issues of November 1981 and January 1982.

[5] See James E. Pesando, "The Indexing of Private Pensions: Separating Fact from Fancy in the Current Debate," mimeo (1978), and "Private Pensions in an Inflationary Climate: Limitations and Policy Alternatives," Economic Council of Canada Discussion Paper No. 114 (April 1978).

[6] Economic Council of Canada, *One In Three: Pensions for Canadians to 2030*, p. 104.

[7] *The Mercer Bulletin*, March 1978.

[8] Ibid.

[9] Arthur W. Donner, "Public and Private Pension Funds and the Competition for Canadian Savings in the 1980's" (Paper prepared for Research Securities of Canada Ltd., Toronto, March 1980), p. 19.

[10] Ibid., p. 12.

[11] The actual elasticity was 1.18 for the period. See ibid., Table 4.4.

[12] Economic Council of Canada, *One In Three: Pensions for Canadians to 2030*, p. 54.

[13] *The Mercer Bulletin*, January 1980, p. 1.

Conclusion

[1] There are other income policy possibilities that would also result in an immediate scaling down of inflation. In a forthcoming book, Clarence L. Barber and John C.P. McCallum propose a three-year program of wage and price controls patterned after the Anti-Inflation Board plan.

The Canadian Institute for Economic Policy has proposed a six-month price freeze, the control of prices set by the largest 400 to 500 corporations, as well as limits on the earnings of higher-income individuals. See its study, "An Economic Agenda for Today" (February 1, 1982).

[2] Arthur W. Donner and Douglas D. Peters, *The Monetarist Counter-Revolution: A Critique of Canadian Monetary Policy 1975-1979* (Toronto: James Lorimer, 1980), pp. 78-81.

Appendix

[1] Edward P. Neufeld, "The Relative Efficiency of the Canadian Capital Market: The Consequences for Canadian-United States Financial Relations," in The Federal Reserve Bank of Boston, *Canadian-United States Financial Relationships: Proceedings of a Conference Held at Melvin Village, New Hampshire* (September 1971), pp. 100-115.

The Canadian Institute for Economic Policy Series

The Monetarist Counter-Revolution: A Critique of Canadian Monetary Policy 1975-1979
Arthur W. Donner and Douglas D. Peters

Canada's Crippled Dollar: An Analysis of International Trade and Our Troubled Balance of Payments
H. Lukin Robinson

Unemployment and Inflation: The Canadian Experience
Clarence L. Barber and John C.P. McCallum

How Ottawa Decides: Planning and Industrial Policy-Making 1968-1980
Richard D. French

Energy and Industry: The Potential of Energy Development Projects for Canadian Industry in the Eighties
Barry Beale

The Energy Squeeze: Canadian Policies for Survival
Bruce F. Willson

The Post-Keynesian Debate: A Review of Three Recent Canadian Contributions
Myron J. Gordon

Water: The Emerging Crisis in Canada
Harold D. Foster and W.R. Derrick Sewell

The Working Poor: Wage Earners and the Failure of Income Security Policies
David P. Ross

Beyond the Monetarists: Post-Keynesian Alternatives to Rampant Inflation, Low Growth and High Unemployment
Edited by David Crane

The Splintered Market: Barriers to Interprovincial Trade in Canadian Agriculture
R.E. Haack, D.R. Hughes and R.G. Shapiro

168

The Drug Industry: A Case Study of the Effects of Foreign Control on the Canadian Economy
Myron J. Gordon and David J. Fowler

The New Protectionism: Non-Tariff Barriers and Their Effects on Canada
Fred Lazar

Industrial Development and the Atlantic Fishery: Opportunities for Manufacturing and Skilled Workers in the 1980s
Donald J. Patton

Canada's Population Outlook: Demographic Futures and Economic Challenges
David K. Foot

The above titles are available from:

James Lorimer & Company, Publishers
Egerton Ryerson Memorial Building
35 Britain Street
Toronto M5A 1R7, Ontario

169